THE MEETING PLACE

THE MEETING PLACE

QUIET SPIRITUAL PRACTICES *for* DWELLING WITH GOD IN PRAYER

LAURA KAUFFMAN

a division of Baker Publishing Group
Grand Rapids, Michigan

© 2026 by Laura Kauffman, LLC

Published by Baker Books
a division of Baker Publishing Group
Grand Rapids, Michigan
BakerBooks.com

Printed in the United States of America

All rights reserved. No part of this publication may be reproduced, stored in a retrieval system, or transmitted in any form or by any means—for example, electronic, photocopy, recording—without the prior written permission of the publisher. The only exception is brief quotations in printed reviews.

Library of Congress Cataloging-in-Publication Data

Names: Kauffman, Laura author
Title: The meeting place : quiet spiritual practices for dwelling with God in prayer / Laura Kauffman.
Description: Grand Rapids, Michigan : Baker Books, a division of Baker Publishing Group, [2026] | Includes biographical information. | Includes bibliographical references.
Identifiers: LCCN 2026004349 | ISBN 9781540906113 paperback | ISBN 9781493465385 ebook
Subjects: LCSH: Spiritual direction—Christianity | Prayer—Christianity
Classification: LCC BV5053 .K38 2026
LC record available at https://lccn.loc.gov/2026004349

Unless otherwise indicated, Scriptures are taken from the Holy Bible, New International Version®, NIV®. Copyright © 1973, 1978, 1984, 2011 by Biblica, Inc.® Used by permission of Zondervan. All rights reserved worldwide. www.zondervan.com. The "NIV" and "New International Version" are trademarks registered in the United States Patent and Trademark Office by Biblica, Inc.®

Scripture quotations labeled ESV are from the ESV® Bible (The Holy Bible, English Standard Version®), © 2001 by Crossway, a publishing ministry of Good News Publishers. ESV Text Edition: 2025. The ESV text may not be quoted in any publication made available to the public by a Creative Commons license. The ESV may not be translated in whole or in part into any other language. Used by permission. All rights reserved.

Scripture quotations labeled MSG are from *The Message*, copyright © 1993, 2002, 2018 by Eugene H. Peterson. Used by permission of NavPress. All rights reserved. Represented by Tyndale House Publishers.

Scripture quotations labeled TLB are from *The Living Bible*, copyright © 1971 by Tyndale House Foundation. Used by permission of Tyndale House Foundation, Carol Stream, Illinois 60188. All rights reserved.

Cover design by Peter Gloege, Look Design Studio

Baker Publishing Group publications use paper produced from sustainable forestry practices and postconsumer waste whenever possible.

26 27 28 29 30 31 32 7 6 5 4 3 2 1

For Sherri

Smell the sawdust. Feel the timbers.
Imagine the boy at his father's bench,
nails in his mouth, hammer in hand.

What did this child build his family?
A meeting place with sturdy walls,
an oversized table, a quiet garden.

"*House* can be a noun or a verb.
Prayer, as well." He opens the door.
Teach us, Carpenter God, to come home.

CONTENTS

AUTHOR'S NOTE

> I don't know exactly what a prayer is.
> I do know how to pay attention.
>
> Mary Oliver[1]

It's early. From my perch on the back patio, I watch a midwinter world begin to wake up. A bird sings, bright and slow. The sky grows a shade lighter, edging the horizon with a long strip of gold. The remaining stars begin to fade. I grip my coffee mug tightly with both hands, despite the heat that stings my fingers.

On this chilly morning, it's completely still. The woods that run along the east side of our property loom large in the darkness, quiet and deep. This peaceful moment will not last long. Soon, the woods will fill with the bustle of animals: woodpeckers tapping for breakfast, rabbits skittering out of their warrens, deer stretching their long legs in the warming air. But in this stolen hour before the dawn, all is quiet, on the brink of everything.

Inside the house, Chris and the kids snore softly. The dogs sleep in a pile on the bathroom floor, and our iPhones rest on their chargers. It's another peaceful moment I know will not last long. Soon, the day will fill with our own bustle of morning activity: kids mumbling for breakfast, permission slips waiting to be signed, dogs whining to go out. But right now, there is only the chill of the lingering night and a soft, heavy silence.

It's no wonder to me, on mornings like this, that the voice of God is still and small.

Most of my life resembles a whirlwind. I hustle at a breakneck speed, anxious to capitalize on every hour of daylight as I manage track meets, meet writing deadlines, arrange dinners with friends, and catch up on household chores.

I'm not complaining; for the most part, this overflowing life is good. I happily open my hands and calendar to the responsibilities that come from belonging to a church, working hard at my vocation, and raising a family. But I've noticed that, before long, my life of good things runs at a pace that could rival Elijah's whirlwind. God's quiet voice is often muffled in a steady hum of busyness.

Here in the dark morning, as I lean against the porch rail, I am one step removed from the chaos. From this vantage point, I observe it with objective eyes. The sheer volume overwhelms me, but even as the weight of responsibility builds in my chest, I exhale, for there, in the middle of the chaos, is God. Might Elijah envy me—a woman who never has to fear a godless space? I can look at my whirlwind and not be afraid, for there he is. In my chaotic life and on my quiet porch, he calls my name and waits.

As in my day to come, the bustle of my faith will soon begin. Sermons and songs, Bible studies and book clubs, service projects and theology conferences: I gobble them up. In my desire to know God, I stuff my life with "more" until I'm whirlwind-busy and spiritually spent. The quiet voice of God is muffled under a cacophony of good noise.

My coffee has cooled enough to drink, and its steam clouds my vision as I take a sip. It's a small mercy, this blurring of my focus. Thoughts about my schedule slip off into the morning air along with the vapors trailing from my dark roast. The bird calls again, and I sing along, borrowing lyrics from The Porter's Gate: "I want to be where my feet are."[2]

When my editor asked me to write a book about spiritual direction, a prayer-centered relationship in which a trained director and an individual listen together for God, she said, "Not many people in our faith community are familiar with the practice, but I think there's a gift in shared contemplative prayer for this anxious, weary generation."

She was right. In my life, this prayer practice has been my "morning on the patio," a moment to step out of my literal and spiritual overfunctioning to rest in the presence of God. It invites me to be where my feet are, to breathe a little deeper, and to be present to the God who is always present to me.

This book invites you, dear reader, to join me on the patio. It's my way of pulling out a chair, filling your cup, and recounting the goodness of God. In these pages you'll find some historical and theological context for spiritual direction and contemplative prayer, but mostly you'll find stories. The stories are my way of saying, "I have seen the Lord!" (John 20:18).

I warn you now, I'm an unreliable narrator. My life, every minute of it, comes to the page. My race, gender, age, nationality, faith tradition, preferences, hiccups: They're all here. My poet's sensibilities have doubtless added shadows and starlight, shoving me toward grandiose language and a skosh of hyperbole. Also, as a woman in love, objectivity is impossible. Spiritual direction is the meeting place where I've encountered my Beloved, and I'm less interested in academic analysis than the contours of his face.

So if you can forgive me those biases, I hope you'll join me in the stories. After telling the stories, I promise to be useful. At the end of each chapter, I'll provide tools for contemplative prayer that have been meaningful to me. As you explore them, you will be writing alongside me, adding your own words to the book. Together, in these pages, we will trace the movements of the Spirit.

We have seen the Lord. Thanks be to God.

1

DEEP ROOTS

The Heritage of Spiritual Direction

> There is something in us, as storytellers and as listeners to stories, that demands the redemptive act, that demands that what falls at least be offered the chance to be restored.
>
> Flannery O'Connor[1]

When I was a girl, my family loaded up our wood-paneled minivan and drove through the Blue Ridge Mountains of North Carolina to visit my grandmother. As a military family, we moved often, but we never once lived near the corner of the South that she called home. My childhood memories of her and the Carolinas are sparse. Mostly I remember the heat: molasses-heavy, dripping with mosquitoes and pine. I remember playing hopscotch in the cul-de-sac and watching snakes climb the birdfeeder. And I remember the Sunset Garden Memorial Cemetery, where my mother took me to visit her daddy.

"See that pond?" she asked, pointing toward the grove of pines. "That's Grandpa's pond. And see that over there? The third headstone from the dogwood? That's where Lewis is buried. Grandpa and Lewis chose this spot so they could spend eternity sneaking down to the pond to fish."

Years later, on an uncharacteristically gentle April day, I stood on that hill again. We opened up the ground and laid my grandmother's remains inside. Despite my tears, I grinned. Would she keep Grandpa to herself tonight? Or let him and Lewis fish in peace? As we prepared to leave the graveside, an old man I'd never met reached for my wrist. "Did you know Edna and I grew up together?" he asked. "She was a little older than me. She was all pearls and red lipstick. She was the classiest lady I ever met. Oh, and that laugh . . ."

I watched seventy years drop from his face as he recalled his youth: swimming holes, home-cooked meals, and her. My grandmother. As he spoke, I felt something rising in my stomach, something like longing. This man had borne witness to my grandmother's life—to parts of her I had never seen—and for all the joy and adventure of my nomadic life, I longed to discover my roots.

One existential crisis, one pandemic, and one Ancestry.com membership later, I began to fill out the picture of my grandmother's world. I traced her family lines through the hills of Appalachia, followed her from tobacco farms to Neiman Marcus, and learned that she never went anywhere in flats. As I learned about her, I also learned about her people—my people—and I began to see that these people whom I'd never met shaped my entire life. I carried their DNA, values, and history in my skin.

They are my good heritage.

In my late thirties, as I was discovering my ancestral roots, I also embarked on a journey of discovering my spiritual roots. It happened by accident. While I wasn't paying attention, a handful of spiritual practices and contemplative ideas popped up like road signs on a map. A friend invited me to a *lectio divina* prayer night. I ordered a new planner, which arrived with a church calendar inside the front cover. My favorite podcast explored an imaginative contemplation exercise, asking me to consider surprising things like how the world might have smelled to Jesus. These practices were trail markers, catching my attention and coaxing me a little further down the road. They colored in the history of my faith, rooting me in a tradition larger than my own experience.

For years, I'd blandly ignored practices like these. I didn't necessarily have anything against them; they were just unfamiliar. In my young-denomination, evangelical church, these practices simply weren't on the map. These were things that *they*—those other kinds of Christians—observed, not *us*.

In a way, this makes sense. When we talk about church, we think about what is familiar. This is the nature of language; we look for the connection in the concept. If I hear you say "family," I don't think about the concepts of lineage or a culture's social structure. I think of muddy cleats, Gatorade bottles, and the feeling of little arms around my neck. Should you say "church," I don't think of the big-picture movements and theologies in the kingdom of God but of our parking spot under the tree and fresh communion bread. We orient our understanding around what is familiar. Yet the family of God is rich and wide. I wonder what gifts we might miss when we too rigidly guard our boundary lines.

In his mercy, God brought me to something stronger than my protectiveness: longing. And he did it with a text message. My friend Hannah had been meeting with a spiritual director for years, and I loved the stories she told about her experiences in prayer; they sounded slow and spacious, filled with God's specific, personal kindnesses to her. I was charmed and curious about spiritual direction, but in a vague sort of way. Then one morning, she sent me the contact information for her director, Sherri. "Give it a try," she texted, with a thumbs-up emoji. "You're going to like it."

Despite feeling a little sheepish, I gave Sherri a call. She was warm and hospitable, more than happy to explain the nuances of the practice to a complete novice like me. "In direction, we close the door to the busy world and turn our attention to Jesus," Sherri said. "Spiritual direction is a shared prayer practice in which we settle into the presence of God together. There's no rush, no agenda. We listen for the Spirit and follow his lead." As she spoke, I recognized an old, familiar longing—something like homesickness—and trusted the surprising tears in my eyes. "Okay," I said. "Let's give it a shot."

For the next five years, I explored the gifts of spiritual direction with Sherri, first as a directee, then as a spiritual-director-in-training, then as a director myself. As I did, I was delighted to find the contemplative practices (once so unknown to me) felt familiar. In them, I recognized the presence of the God I knew. This meeting place for prayer felt safe, with the Bible as its backbone and the love of Jesus as its heartbeat; it belonged to the family of God. Unaware, I had stumbled upon part of my heritage.

David Benner writes, "Spiritual direction is an ancient form of Christian soul care that goes all the way back to the earliest days of the church. It has never really gone away. It is just that large sectors of the Christian church have forgotten their own heritage."[2] As I learned about spiritual direction, God drew my eyes backward along the family tree of faith, beyond the scope of my own experience, denomination, and even century. The practice wends through church history like a thread, weaving all the way back to the very pages of the Word of God. Directors often point to Ananias and Paul, Peter and Cornelius, and even Jesus and his disciples for precedent.

In many ways, the biblical story of Samuel and Eli in 1 Samuel 3 captures the essence of spiritual direction. It starts with a moment to which every parent can relate: a small voice at the edge of the bed calling out in the middle of the night, "I'm here! What is it?" I imagine Eli, the bleary-eyed priest, confused. *Did I groan? Make a noise in my sleep?* "No. Sorry. Go back to bed. I didn't call you."

The boy shuffles back to his room, the priest drops back to sleep, and the night returns to normal. Until . . . "I'm here! You called me."

No one knows the exact moment Eli realized the voice in the dark wasn't the creation of a child's nightmare or the aching groans of an old man's sleep. We simply know that he knew. There, in the darkest hours of the night, Eli recognized the presence of the Divine. The old priest coached Samuel on what to do next: "Go, lie down, and wait. If he calls again, say, 'Speak, Lord. Your servant is listening.'"

God didn't descend with power or a proclamation, though he had every right to do so. He didn't force himself or impose. He simply called Samuel's name and waited.

Spiritual direction—mercifully and scandalously—hinges on the theological assumptions that God is calling to us, that he wants to be known, and that all we have to do is respond. Following in the footsteps of Eli, a director helps a person pay attention to the movements of God in their own life and experience. By listening compassionately, the director cultivates a safe space in which a person can meet with God.

While this practice has its roots in Scripture, it more officially took shape in the third century with the desert mothers and fathers. This group of early believers—disillusioned with the distractions and corruptions of everyday life—retreated to the desert to create communities centered on prayer, simplicity, and faith. People would travel from surrounding areas to meet with these cloistered believers and receive guidance in matters of the Spirit.

As time passed, the world, the church, and the practice of spiritual direction evolved. Wars were won and lost, societies became interconnected, and the church branched into varied denominations and structures. Through it all, the practice of spiritual direction bloomed differently in each branch of the family of God. It continued to weave through church history until it blossomed with a huge resurgence in the 1980s.

As I traced the thread of this practice through denominations and divisions, I found familiar faces: John Calvin and Martin Luther, Teresa of Ávila and Ignatius of Loyola, Henri Nouwen and Eugene Peterson. Seeing their connection with spiritual direction felt anchoring, like running into an old friend while traveling. "You're here too? Tell me what you think!" When I found out C. S. Lewis had seen a spiritual director for over a decade, I started to get serious about giving this whole thing a try. After all, I'd follow that man to Narnia and back.

The church has a myriad of soul-care tools to help its members grow. While most share a foundation of overarching beliefs, each has its own emphasis. Bible study strengthens the mind. Discipleship strengthens the will. Counseling strengthens the heart. Liturgy strengthens the habits.

There is a sort of holy osmosis that happens in these practices. As we study, our hearts wake up as well as our minds. As we obey, the truths of the Word become embodied, more lived than understood. As we care for our hearts, our habits shift to reflect our healing. We are holistic beings, after all. The nourishment we provide to one part of ourselves blesses the whole.

The same kind of holy osmosis occurs with spiritual direction. While it is not a tool for Bible study, it often explores the Word. While it is not focused on personal growth, it often changes our behavior. While it is not a vehicle for therapy, it often stirs our hearts. At its core, spiritual direction is a practice of communion. It tends to the relational aspect of our faith, drawing us ever deeper into a lived experience of the heart of God.

When my children were small—the youngest a baby and the oldest maybe five—I introduced them to the beach. We're a Midwest family, so there wasn't a lot of fodder for their imaginations when it came to the Atlantic. Trying to describe the ocean to them, I started conceptually. "Okay. The ocean is a big body of water that separates continents." Blank stares. Then (predictably) questions about what a continent was and how water ended up getting a body.

I tried again, this time a little more practically. "So. It moves in waves . . . well, except when it doesn't. It's blue . . . and green . . . and white . . . and sometimes, the sun makes it look yellow and orange."

Obviously, that didn't help.

"Okay," I said. "How about this? It's the place where dolphins live and pirates sail. The waves have special voices, some that lull you to sleep and some that make your heart beat fast. There are places in the middle of the ocean that no one has ever been. You'll run, splash, float, and swim in it. Sometimes, you'll use the water to build castles and kingdoms of seashells. Other times, you'll just sit and watch it roll. Trust me, you're going to like it."

Better. They still had no idea what I was talking about, but now they knew one thing: They wanted it. It turns out that mystery and beauty don't lend themselves to an elevator pitch. Words will only get you so far; at the end of the day, you have to spend some time at the beach.

Much like the ocean, the process of spiritual direction isn't easy to distill. Its cornerstones—relationship, prayer, and the Holy Spirit—are dynamic. Information alone won't do justice to the mystery and beauty of cultivating intimacy with God, never mind checklists and formulas. But the rhythms of contemplative prayer can serve as our oars, helping us paddle deeper into connection with God.

PRACTICE: STORYWORK

Humans are storytelling creatures. Stories help us make sense of the world, connect with others, and access emotions. Jesus modeled storytelling throughout the Gospels, often responding to demands for theological clarity with narratives.

In the same way a parable helps us process spiritual truth, Storywork helps us make sense of our lives while opening rich ground in prayer. This practice begins by asking God to guide our attention through different seasons of our lives. While the events of our past don't change, our experience of telling them does. As we pray through this exercise, we simply notice what we notice, trusting God will highlight the specific parts of our story he wants us to remember today.

Whatever comes to mind, rest in the knowledge that Jesus knows you, loves you, and will meet you in every chapter of your life. To explore your story is to find him in it.

1. **Prepare.** Grab a pen and paper. Find a quiet place where you won't be interrupted. Before you begin, take a moment to be present. Notice the sounds in

the room. Take a deep breath. Enjoy a few moments of stillness.*

2. **Pray.** When you are ready, become aware of God's presence with you. Ask the Spirit to guide your attention as you reflect on your story.
3. **Remember.** Start at the beginning. Make notes about your childhood. Let your senses wake up. What smells and sounds do you remember? What toys or textures come to mind? Notice what you notice and write it down.
4. **Outline.** As you reflect on your life, you might like to outline significant moments or events. You can use decades (twenties, thirties, forties, etc.) or locations to help you organize your timeline. Don't worry about capturing every detail; just notice what stands out today.
5. **Consider.** As you survey your timeline, consider your spiritual formation. How has your family (especially your family of origin) molded your faith? What life events have affected how you interact with God?
6. **End.** As you close your reflection, notice which stories and memories grab your attention. Invite Jesus to have the final word. Perhaps he wants you to see something new. Perhaps there's an old wound that needs some care. Perhaps you sense God's presence in your story in a different way. Close your time in prayer by inviting him to speak.

*Or not. I have three sons. This "quiet, uninterrupted place" does not exist in my house. Don't let that stop you. Do this exercise at the dinner table while the kids wrestle on the floor. Jot down notes in the school pickup line. Reflect on life while the grandkids fingerpaint from your sofa. God is with you always, even to the end of the decibel scale.

7. **Share.** Consider sharing your story with a spiritual director (who will help you notice and name the gifts of God, or "gather the graces," and track God's movements in your life) or with a friend who can be trusted to listen compassionately.

2

PRESENT TO THE PRESENCE

Settling into Contemplative Prayer

> The most holy and necessary practice in our spiritual life is the presence of God.
>
> Brother Lawrence[1]

I have this little ritual I enact before each spiritual direction session. It starts with removing the taxidermy deer from the office wall. My husband and I share the space, so before hosting an hour of prayer, I tuck "Granddaddy" away in the bedroom while Chris rolls his eyes and tells me not to muss up his fur. I roll my eyes back, insisting that no one could pray under that dead-eyed stare. He assures me this is not the case, but nevertheless, I persist.

After Granddaddy is squirreled away, I pull out the branching candelabra we got as a wedding gift. I strike a match, hold it to the three tall tapers, and say, "I light these candles to remind myself that I am in the presence of the Father, the Son, and the Holy Spirit."

This simple phrase reminds me that prayer is not a locked room. No magic combination of silence or attention will open the door to the Holy of Holies; that curtain was torn down long ago. I don't need to attain the presence of God because, as Richard Rohr writes, I am already in the presence of God.[2] All that is needed is awareness. So I watch the flames, exhale, and remember.

Soon, the person I'm meeting with (the directee) will arrive, and I'll greet them at the door with a cup of coffee and two of the world's largest dogs. We'll chitchat our way to the office before locking out the dogs and the rest of the loud, distracting world. They will plop into one of the oversized leather chairs and drop their bag on the floor. Then, the second part of my ritual begins.

"I am glad you are here," I will say. "Now, let's start by taking a moment to settle in."

Almost without fail, the first place this invitation lands is in the directee's body. Shoulders drop. Eyes close. Breaths grow deep. In my quiet office, with its view of the prairie and the wild Iowa sky, all is still. With our bodies and silence, we join them. Cell phones are turned off, day planners are closed, and for one short hour, we consent to be nowhere else. We are simply here, in the present moment, with God and each other.

There is something radically intentional about pausing long enough to say, "Yes. I am here, and I consent to be." It's powerful in the context of spiritual direction, and it's holy work in the ordinary moments of life as well. Whether I'm rocking a feverish child in the middle of the night or sipping a glass of wine at sunset, being present to the moment is an act of awareness and trust.

But it isn't easy. Honestly, I'm a bit out of practice; I blame my phone (my favorite scapegoat of the moment). With its little alerts and dopamine hits, it lures me into another world. Before long, I'm driving *and* responding to phone calls, having dinner *and* reading the news, chatting with a friend *and* checking my text notifications. I'm no longer in one moment; I'm in fifteen of them. The attention economy fights for my interest, and it doesn't take long before I'm willing to surrender to its distractions so I can escape the boredom of a checkout line or the discomfort of a sleepless night.

While I'm not ready to step off my technology soapbox yet, I know there are merits to our connected world. I can set down my megaphone long enough to find gratitude. But still, I notice that I feel a bit like Bilbo Baggins at the beginning of *The Fellowship of the Ring*: "thin, sort of stretched . . . like butter that has been scraped over too much bread."[3] In the buzzing distractions of my day, the richness and flavor of life can get diluted. I long for a quiet space to be fully present to myself and the still small voice of God.

On a bright winter day, one of my directees shared the perfect metaphor for this tension. Gazing at the icy world outside my window, she said, "I think this is the only time this month I've slowed down. I feel like my life is happening nonstop. It's like a telemarketer headset—you know the kind I mean? You have a queue of people on the line, waiting to be connected. When you finish one call, there's immediately a new person in your ear, no lag time. You're constantly responding to the things that pop up. That is what my life feels like." She spun her wrist in the air like she was flipping an invisible Rolodex. "One thing after another after another."

Even as she said it, I felt the resonance in my spirit. *I know that feeling.* My calendar fights against the empty space, as does my inner taskmaster. When moments of stillness present themselves, I don't usually feel relief—I feel guilt. Can I justify taking a break when the floor is covered in muddy dog prints, my prayer journal hasn't been opened in days, and the kids will be eating celery for dinner if I don't make a trip to the store? *I'll rest when all the work is done*, I think, ignoring the niggling doubt in the back of my mind that the work will ever be done.

A few weeks ago, when my computer chimed with a reminder that my director, Sherri, would call soon, I groaned. Don't get me wrong—I (obviously) love spiritual direction, but the hour I had set aside to pray was coming at a terrible time. On this particular day, the list of things I had to accomplish was monumental. It was the sort of day that makes a shower feel indulgent, so the thought of breaking stride to pray felt more disorienting than helpful.

For a second, I considered canceling the session, but only for a second. If years of spiritual direction have taught me anything, it's that God is kind. He doesn't need me to tug on my spiritual bootstraps and bring my A-game to prayer. He just needs me to come. So when my laptop pinged on the desk, I adjusted a few unruly curls, turned on my Zoom camera, and thought, *Well, here we go anyway.*

Ever since our initial call years ago, Sherri has been my spiritual director. I wish everyone could have a Sherri. Her love for Jesus is an ocean. Her generosity flows in fresh bread and baked oatmeal, and her tendency to laugh uproariously at inappropriate moments is utterly endearing. While there are countless things I could tell you about Sherri, her whole person can be summed up in this: She is a friend of Jesus. You can tell; he hangs all over her.

Sherri has been a faithful friend through seasons that score a ten on the intensity meter—cancer scares, risky surgeries, unexpected layoffs—and through seasons of the mundane, when I show up for direction thinking, *Huh. I have no idea what to pray about today.* She has seen me at my best, and she has seen me at my worst. It would take much more than a distracted, grouchy attitude to put her off.

When her face popped up on the screen, I knew I had made a good choice, but I still had no idea what to talk about. Some days, prayer refuses to confine itself to language.

"Laura, it's so good to see you." Sherri grinned. "I'm excited to spend this time with you and Jesus today. Let's pray and get you settled in."

With a roll of my neck and a deep breath, I closed my eyes. *Okay*, I thought, *okay. Be here. You don't have to drive the bus right now.* It's a silly phrase, but in that moment, it was a surrender. Releasing the reins of control of my life (and of prayer) felt like an exhale.

After a minute, Sherri prayed over me, as she always does. She named the same reality I honor with the rustic candelabra in my office: We are in the presence of the God of the universe, and that God is looking on us—on me—with unchanging, incomprehensible love.

"We ask for the grace of awareness," she prayed. "May Laura experience your loving gaze upon her. As she takes as much silence as she needs, we ask that you bless her with the sense of your nearness."

Then we were still.

The silence that followed was heavy and deep. I didn't hear voices from on high or receive floods of insight, but there in the quiet, Jesus was with me. He didn't say a word, and he didn't expect me to. The only thing that mattered was that we were there together.

Max Lucado retells the famous story of a reporter who once asked Mother Teresa what she says to God when she prays. "I listen," she answered. Following up, the reporter continued, "Well, then, what does God say?" With a smile, she simply replied, "He listens."[4]

There are no words for how that deep, listening silence of God tended to me during that session. The tears and minutes flowed unchecked as the God of Love ministered to my overfunctioning, disconnected soul—not with language but with presence. He cared for me in ways I didn't know I needed. He unwound me. Prayer was no longer one more activity on a spiritual checklist. It ceased to be a verb—an action I accomplished—and became a noun. Prayer was a meeting place. It was home.

And Sherri? Sherri set the table for connection and guarded the door of our silence. She created space for me to enter Sabbath stillness with God.

In his beautiful work *Sabbath as Resistance*, Walter Brueggemann describes Sabbath as an invitation to receptivity in which "what is needed is given and need not be seized."[5] Any kid who has counted the days to Christmas morning can tell you that receiving is great, but it's also vulnerable. To receive, our hands must be open—not working, protecting, or offering anything. They are simply exposed and waiting. Who can say what will be placed into them? And when?

To enter into the practice of stillness with God, even in the short transition into spiritual direction, is a beautiful and radical act of trust. It turns time into a feat of surrender. With our hands and our minds, we acknowledge that we are not in control, that deep down we really don't want to be, and that the work belongs to God. In stillness, we cultivate faith.

So yes, stillness is vulnerable. And yes, we never know exactly what we will find there. But thank God, we always know *who* we will find there. Whatever fear, shame, doubt, anger, or boredom meets us in the quiet, all will be well, for God is there too, with love so strong it can't be quenched by the finality of death or the mundanity of life, by our better angels or our darkest impulses, by our present reality or our future uncertainties. Nothing will be able to keep us from his love—not power, distance, or anything else in all of creation—including, thank God, ourselves.

Back in my office, with those tall tapers burning, I bring my ritual to a close. A little time has passed. We have slowed down and oriented ourselves to the loving gaze of our Maker. We remember that God is with us now and always, in the quiet and the chaos.

Together, in the soft light, we direct our eyes toward the third chair in the room. I leave it empty, but as you can probably guess, it is never empty. It just takes us a moment to remember, so we open our hands and receive.

PRACTICE: LETTING GOD LOOK AT YOU

In the Old Testament, Hagar named God El Roi, saying, "You are the God who sees me" (Gen. 16:13). Moments before this tender proclamation, she had been living in one of the darkest chapters of her story, one defined by abuse, neglect, and ultimately abandonment. Alone in the desert, running from her abuser, she may have believed no one in the world cared for her, not even God. But there, in that desolate place, the Lord "found her" and tended to her. Hagar's circumstances didn't immediately change, but it didn't matter. She knelt on the ground, naming it holy, saying, "I have now seen the One who sees me." The loving gaze of God changed everything.

One of the sweetest, simplest ways to begin prayer is to let God look at you. In the Spiritual Exercises, Ignatius of Loyola encourages us to practice sitting under the loving gaze of God, imagining the Trinity watching us with unchanging love and delight. This practice is a quiet consent, an act of being present to the God who is present to us. Few practices have tended to my heart like this one.*

*Be sure to give yourself grace as you practice. If you sense God's loving gaze, wonderful. Enjoy that sensation. If the practice feels flat, don't worry. Sometimes

1. **Pause.** Wherever you are (whether you're sitting in a prayer room or waiting at a stoplight), pause. Breathe deeply. Let your mind and body be still for just a moment.
2. **Notice.** Become aware that you are in the presence of God and that he is looking at you with love. If it's helpful, repeat this phrase in rhythm with your breath: "I am in the presence (inhale) of God's loving gaze (exhale)."
3. **Imagine.** Let your imagination explore the reality that God is looking at you, right here, right now. What does his gaze feel like? What does his face look like?
4. **Enjoy.** Rest in the warmth of his love. When you are satisfied, you might repeat Hagar's blessing: "I have now seen the One who sees me."

---

it's easy; sometimes it's a discipline. It doesn't matter. Whatever we experience, the truth remains: God sees and loves us, whether we sense it or not.

3

BE STILL

Spiritual Direction as Sabbath

> We know what to do with space, but how do we shape sacred time?
>
> Susannah Heschel[1]

In the final year of my counseling graduate program, I sat in the brightly lit waiting room of the program director, Tammy. It was spring. The office walls were high and white. The massive windows cast a warm glow over the leather chairs and the cheery office manager. The building smelled old, like history and a few too many rainstorms. It was a place that begged you to shut off your phone, brew a cup of chamomile, and pull a book off the shelf. On that spring day, however, a pleasure read was the last thing on my mind.

My knees bounced as I thumbed at the corners of the manila folders on my lap. I checked my watch, impatient.

One of my favorite parts of being a graduate assistant was my weekly supervision session with Tammy. She had a way of listening that slowed time. When she leaned in and looked at me, I knew she was hearing more than I was saying.

Usually, when I camped out in the leather chairs to wait for our meeting, my mind began to slow down. But on this day, my thoughts darted to my upcoming psychopharmacology exam, psychotherapy and trauma presentation, three internship counseling sessions, and evening substance abuse recovery group. As I waited for Tammy, I chugged a second espresso and tapped a cadence of anxiety on the old wood floor.

Exactly as the clock struck two, Tammy rounded the corner. Despite my stress, I grinned. Maybe it was from her years playing water polo or the resilience gained from winters spent in Winnipeg, but she had a presence. She moved like someone entirely at home in her body.

I must have had a way of carrying myself as well, because Tammy took one look at me with my red eyes and clenched jaw and said, "Right. Supervision time. Come with me." To my surprise, she led me away from her office's throw pillows and soft lighting and to a rarely used storage room at the end of the hall. She turned to me and held out her hand. "Bags."

I followed her every command like a child. I gave her all I had with me: cell phone, manila folders, textbooks, day planner. Satisfied, she nodded and pointed to the couch in the corner of the room.

"Today, your work is to rest," she said, as I sat down. "I'll wake you when the hour is over." With a reassuring smile, she flipped off the light and closed the door.

I sat blinking in the dark, baffled by the sudden change in speed. Tentatively, I lay back on the couch and reached for a blanket, testing the waters of rest. My thoughts whirled around me in the dark. I was like a skateboard with too much momentum; my foot might not be pushing the pavement of achievement anymore, but my wheels were still spinning.

Against my clenched eyelids, I watched a slideshow of my to-do list. There was so much good work to be done: people in pain, legitimate evil to fight, the kingdom coming. The images pulled at me, beckoning me to abandon my place on the couch and return to the day's demands.

The work wasn't the only thing that pulled at me. Shame, which I found deeply embedded underneath my to-dos, rattled in my mind as well. In all my busy activity, I hadn't noticed that shame—and its cousin, fear—were whispering their mantras in the back of my mind:

Other people can hack this. Why can't you? What's wrong with you?

They're going to see through you. You don't deserve to be here. There's no place for you.

Think of the damage you'll cause if you do this wrong.

In the dark, I closed my eyes tighter, trying to fight the lies. *Please*, I prayed, with a deep breath. *Jesus*. In and out, over and over, I said those two small words in the dark. Deep, fresh mouthfuls of air led me away from the narratives of shame and settled me at the feet of Jesus. My poor, overworked mind didn't have to formulate fancy prayers. I didn't have to muster up the spiritual resolve to assess my needs, read my Bible, or journal my inner desires. All I had to do was breathe Jesus's name until everything else grew soft around the edges, intangible.

And there, in the chaotic, shame-filled, caffeine-fueled dark, I drifted off to sleep.

In her book *Sacred Rhythms*, Ruth Haley Barton writes,

> Most of us are more tired than we know at the soul level. We are teetering on the brink of dangerous exhaustion, and we really cannot do anything else until we have gotten some rest. . . . We really can't engage [any spiritual disciplines] until solitude becomes a place of rest for us rather than another place for human striving and hard work.[2]

On that spring day in graduate school, Tammy knew the spiritual disciplines I needed were rest and solitude, but it was costly for her to offer them. During our supervision sessions, she reviewed student files, taught me valuable skills, and assessed the quality of my work. While I rested, those things went undone. To me, that felt like failure. I needed her steady, rooted presence to remind me that I was more than my accomplishments. I needed Tammy to be my Jethro.

Jethro, Moses's father-in-law, only appears a few times in the Exodus narrative, but his wisdom shapes the entire book. To set the scene for Jethro's arrival, imagine the hyper-busy, put-upon Moses of Exodus 18. The plagues and miracles have passed; the Israelites have crossed the Red Sea and entered the wilderness. Our slave-turned-prince-turned-fugitive has seen more in the last few months than most people see in a lifetime: hailstorms and blood waters, exposed riverbeds and armies of drowned corpses, fiery columns and smoke in the sky. Can you imagine the effect that has on the nervous system?

As if that was not enough, there are two million or so shell-shocked, emotionally spent Israelite refugees waiting for him with important questions like "Where is the bathroom?" and "What's for dinner?"

The people are free, but skirmishes break out. Scarcity mindset and trauma responses linger, even in the light of salvation. And so we find Moses sitting with his father-in-law. Jethro looks at the people who have been surrounding Moses since dawn with their all-too-legitimate needs.

"What is this that you are doing for the people?" Jethro asks Moses. "Why do you sit alone, and all the people stand around you from morning till evening?" (v. 14 ESV). Moses splutters, explaining the importance of his work—he is the intermediary between God and the people. The older, wiser Jethro replies with, I like to imagine, a dismissive wave of the hand. "Bah. My advice? Delegate."

We all need a voice like Jethro's. The pull of responsibility tugs on us all. It stayed with me far beyond that spring day in the storage closet. As a young mom with Cheerios in my hair and Curious George in my purse, I've carried the weight of raising precious souls. As a counselor with a full client load, I've carried the weight of walking with others through unimaginable pain and loss. As a wife, friend, daughter, writer, Christian, and American, I've shouldered still more responsibilities.

Tammy was my Jethro that day in graduate school, and as the years passed, I needed the voice of a Jethro again, reminding me to take my place in the order of things.

When I first met with Sherri, she warned me that I might fall asleep. "Don't worry," she said, and laughed at my horror-struck face. "I'll nudge you if you start snoring." At the time, I couldn't imagine a scenario in which I fell asleep during spiritual direction. After all, I'd decided to meet with Sherri because I wanted to do things: discernment, repentance, inspiration, growth. Of all the work I thought my soul needed, sleep wasn't on the list.

In our first session, Sherri led me into prayer by reminding me to catch my breath. "You are in the presence of God. Let your body and mind settle as you breathe in his love." I took a deep breath and remembered that dark storage closet. My spiritual ambitions fell away. I settled into God's loving presence and let him take the lead. Now, every month when I meet with Sherri, she is my Jethro, ignoring my protests of importance and inviting me to balance.

For the hour I meet with her, I am drawn out of the rolling cadence of time and reminded that rest is an act of freedom. Time becomes a temple. I set aside my to-do lists and the lies productivity whispers about my value. In the quiet, I position myself not to produce but to receive. In its rhythm of rest, spiritual direction becomes a Sabbath practice.

Of all the commandments Moses brought down from the mountain, the Sabbath might seem the most anachronistic. Many of the commands (don't murder, don't steal, don't covet) are pretty straightforward. We contextualize them easily; the nightly news provides documentary evidence of what goes wrong when violence, violation, and greed run rampant. But keeping Sabbath is a little trickier to wrap our minds around, especially in a cultural climate that sets productivity as the standard for value.

In the order of the commandments, Old Testament scholars note something interesting in the placement of the Sabbath. Right there between the love-of-God commands (1–3) and the love-of-neighbor commands (5–10) hangs the

Sabbath, like a bridge.[3] What if that order isn't arbitrary but invitational? Might Sabbath rest be the result of loving God and the fuel for loving others?

When a spiritual direction session begins with silence, we place ourselves right in the middle of the Ten Commandments. As the first three instruct, we acknowledge God as our first, our only, and our honored Beloved. Then? We rest. Is there good spiritual work to come in our hour together? Probably. But whatever lies ahead, we begin here, *on the bridge* between the love of God and others.

For the final time, I'm back with Moses. I imagine him beleaguered and weary, walking up the thundering mountain. Did he drag his feet as he went? As I watch him climb into the dark cloud, I know what's coming: the Ten Commandments, the Glory, the golden calf.

In between its cinematic moments, the book of Exodus lays out chapters—*chapters*—of instructions for the freed nation. God is establishing a new world order. There are civil laws about land allocation, restitution, and social justice. There are religious laws so intricate they detail the needlework pomegranates on the priests' robes and the measurements of cassia in the temple incense. In a dramatic escape story that takes forty chapters to tell, God's meticulous instructions take eleven of them.

God concludes his commands to Moses by saying, "According to all that I have commanded you, [the people] shall do" (Exod. 31:11 ESV). The God of the Quaking Mountain has given the Israelites a job; we can tell the work matters by the sheer virtue of the attention God gives it. The work, however, is not all he commands.

God tells Moses, "You are to speak to the people of Israel and say, '*Above all* you shall keep my Sabbaths, for this is a sign between me and you throughout your generations, that you may know that I, the LORD, sanctify you. . . . It is a sign forever between me and the people of Israel that in six days the LORD made the heavens and the earth, and on the seventh day he rested and was refreshed" (vv. 13, 17 ESV, emphasis mine).

Above all, he said. Eleven chapters of instructions, but above all—Sabbath.

Sabbath rest, the tabernacle in time, was the sign that the Israelites belonged to God. Their days were not measured in output or weighed in fear. Like a wedding ring, Sabbath rest symbolized that the people were joined to the God of freedom. By entering his rest, they agreed, "It is he, the Lord, who sanctifies."

Did they have good work to do? Yes. Did it matter? Yes. But did the work itself sanctify them? No. No, it did not, nor did their ability to keep his covenant or establish his kingdom. When we follow their lead and choose to enter Sabbath rest, we stand with the freed Israelites and cast our eyes ahead to the cross, agreeing, "Indeed. It is finished."

PRACTICE: BREATH PRAYER

This practice is as simple and refreshing as a good deep breath. In this form of contemplative prayer, we repeat a short phrase in rhythm with our inhale and exhale. It's a way of praying without ceasing and letting our bodies participate in the conversation with God. The steady rhythm of breathing becomes the metronome for prayer.

The most well-known breath prayer, "The Jesus Prayer," is derived from Luke 18 and offers a variation on the tax collector's chest-pounding plea: "Lord Jesus Christ / have mercy on me."

At night, when I have trouble sleeping, I pray a version of Psalm 4:8: "In peace I will lie down and sleep, / for you alone, Lord, make me dwell in safety." In times of suffering, my prayer is more straightforward and raw: "Oh, my God / please help."

Whatever phrase you use, rest in the promise that he is close to you, as close as a breath.

1. **Begin.** Choose a phrase: a Bible verse, a prayer request, or a promise. Shorter is better.

2. **Settle.** Enter prayer, knowing God is with you. Notice your weight in the chair, your feet on the floor. Orient your spirit to God's nonanxious presence.
3. **Breathe.** Notice the quality of the air. What does it feel like on your lips or nostrils? Does your chest move? Your belly? Inhale. Exhale.
4. **Recite.** When you are ready, repeat your phrase in rhythm with your breath. Let your inhale and exhale draw you deeper in.
5. **Pray.** You'll get distracted. When your thoughts drift off (and they will), hold that with kindness. Simply notice that you've wandered off and gently bring your attention back to God and your breath. Return to your phrase and repeat it for at least seven breath cycles.
6. **Close.** When you are satisfied, close your prayer by noticing what (if anything) shifted in your body, mind, or spirit. Whatever you notice, be at peace. As we breathe in God's truth, it becomes part of us. With every breath, we anchor ourselves in his slow, steady work.

4

AT HOME

The Self and Spiritual Direction

> There are no unsacred places.
>
> Wendell Berry[1]

Growing up as a military kid isn't for everyone, but it suited me down to the ground. Every few years, our family received orders to pack our belongings, say goodbye to our friends, and travel across the country to start a new life. The rhythm of these departures didn't bother me. My parents, sister, and I were close; they were home to me, more than four walls ever could be. While I did miss things like favorite climbing trees or big bedroom windows, I developed a nomad's spirit. After a few years in a new location, my feet would start to itch, and wanderlust would draw my eyes to the horizon.

So it surprised me, as an adult, to find myself daydreaming about a permanent home. I imagined a place where I could mark my sons' heights on the doorframe and eat apples from trees I had planted. Maybe one day, I could slice a Honeycrisp for my grandchildren and mark their heights on the wall beside their fathers'. No place had ever held both my history and future, but I started envisioning one that could. Chris and I knew it wouldn't be a place in the suburbs (we aren't well suited for concrete), so we began to hunt for a patch of wild earth to call home.

After a few years of searching, we found it. We stumbled across the listing online and eagerly drove out of the city and into the hills that run along the western border of the state. The house rested in a high spot in a valley. On the day we visited, the wrens were in fine form, singing from the dappled light of the cottonwood trees. Crickets leaped from the prairie grasses, following us down the path to the camping area and fire pit. A stream fed a little pond and turned the ground around the oaks into a marshy pool. My youngest son slipped his hand in mine and announced that he would call this "the heavenly place." True to form, I cried.

The property was full of surprises. Spring taught us that black-eyed Susans and purple coneflowers bloomed in the lane behind the house. A family of swallows nested under the patio and swooped around our heads in the evening, catching dragonflies and mosquitoes. Less charming, the basement put out a funky smell, the source of which we still haven't been able to find.

We moved into a home with a history. Fifteen years before, Susan and Bob picked out a plot of land on an old beet farm, called in a builder, and laid the frame of what would be our eventual home. They lived there happily for years until Susan started going blind from all the light. With no small amount of sorrow, they handed us the keys and moved into town.

Not long after we moved in, I got a text from Susan. She had ordered blackberry bushes in bulk from an online retailer and was convinced the leftovers would thrive on our hill behind the chicken coop. Gratefully, I penciled in the date for her visit and tilled up a patch of chicken-pecked soil.

Susan's visits were always a treat. Not only was she generous and gentle but she was full of stories about the property. We learned that the hallways stretched double the usual width to accommodate Susan's aging mother. "She hated the thought that she was slowing everyone up with her walker. We didn't want her to have to rush."

Once, Susan pointed at the wall of windows that reached from the vaulted ceiling to the basement. "The light was for the grandbabies. They were so scared of the dark," she muttered, almost to herself. "We can't let the babies be afraid of the dark. Not in my house."

For years, Susan came by every time the season changed. She wanted to see how her mother's memorial tree was faring and if the ducks had returned to the pond. She came for years—until one year she didn't. Some losses don't get easier.

Susan doesn't visit anymore, but the house continues to tell secrets. It's ours, but it's not ours. We tend to it, but we don't fully understand it. It's a product of the couple who crafted it. Every wildflower or oddly placed window whispers their names.

I feel a little silly rhapsodizing about the property, but I think I'm in good company. In the psalms, David marvels at his home in the world with a similar grandiosity. In Psalm

19, he looks at the wild night sky and says, "The heavens declare the glory of God, and the sky above proclaims his handiwork. Day to day pours out speech, and night to night reveals knowledge" (vv. 1–2 ESV). Like an art student in front of "The Starry Night," David traces the strokes of creation, letting the canvas teach him about the Artist.

About a hundred psalms later, we find David marveling again. "Your works are wonderful," he writes. "I know that full well" (Ps. 139:14). But this time, David isn't gazing at a starry night sky or over the Iowa prairie—he's looking at himself. Unafraid of specificity, he praises the intricacies of his body, the days of his life, and even his kidneys.[2] David knew God's glory was not confined to the Milky Way or mighty rushing waters; the glory of God was on display in his skin.

If I'm being honest, part of me envies David's chutzpah. Rarely do I look at my sagging stomach, use of time, and worried heart, and think, *Wow. Good job, God. You did wonderful work with me.*

More often, I survey myself with the eye of a contractor appraising a fixer-upper. What needs to be spackled? What is underperforming and proving expensive? Where did those leaks come from? I look at my body, my time, and my emotions with a critical eye.

I forget that I am not my own. Instead of considering what my life says about my Creator, I focus on what it says about me, which usually isn't good. I can be so self-critical, so sin-obsessed, so scared of the dark in me; I need the eyes of Susan, the builder, to let in some light and say, "We can't let the babies be afraid of the dark. Not in my house."

A few years back, the state of Iowa sent an arborist, Lindsey, to coach us through a prairie restoration project designed to revive the natural habitats lost to subdivisions and cattle. As the prairies became populated, developers brought in wild honeysuckles to fill the ditches and fast-growing brome to feed the cows. Though well-intended, these plants turned out to be voracious and invasive, crowding out natural grasses and trees. The state offered funds (and, even more valuably, advice) to homeowners who want to restore their land to its native condition.

Lindsey met us in the front yard with a clipboard and muck boots. As we climbed the ridge behind the black locusts, she taught us about the land. "It'll be tricky to get much to grow on the slope over there," she said as she pointed. "Cottonwoods are your best bet." She knelt and ran her hands through the dirt. "And this? There's a good bit of clay in this part of the soil. Best to try something like big bluestem." She stood up and brushed her hands on her overalls. "If you want to grow anything good, you have to know your ground."

Somewhere along the way, in my stream of faith, the idea of knowing the ground of ourselves eroded. Perhaps fearing the invasive weeds of self-obsession and sin justification, we stopped looking at our bodies, hearts, and minds as precious ground. In the name of well-intended repentance, we turned a critical gaze toward our flesh, thoughts, desires, and emotional lives. We viewed ourselves with an appraiser's eye and an endless drive to fill the ditches. No longer were we stewards of the beautiful but "flippers" of the flawed.

Don't misunderstand—the work of repentance and right living matters. Some legitimate weeds need to be torn from the beds of our faith. Repentance is as vital to the health of the soul as cutting down honeysuckle is for the health of the forest. But perhaps, in our efforts to work the ground, we've forgotten it was first called good.

To know our ground, we must begin at the beginning. The Bible sets the scene; in the Genesis narrative, we hear the first echoes of birdsong, see the first beads of crystalline dew, and watch the first creatures stretch in the morning sun.

Our story begins here, on this perfect morning in the garden. God kneels among the lilacs and bumblebees and (perhaps a bit like Lindsey) rakes his fingers through the dirt. He turns the soil over in his hands, reaching for more, feeling its coolness against his palm. What did it smell like as he held it to his face and breathed? After touching the lips of God, is it any wonder that the soil became human? I imagine God sitting back on his heels, muddy palms on his knees, saying, "Oh yes. Very good."

We all know the next part of the story. Before long, "Very good" will turn into "Where are you?" The snake. The fruit. The fig leaves. The story doesn't need retelling; we carry it in our skin.

Mercifully, the story progresses. We know the cross is coming, making all the brokenness (in the words of Sally Lloyd-Jones) "come untrue."[3] In his life, death, and resurrection, Jesus crushes the head of sin and clothes us in garments of redemption.

When we tell our story, do we begin with the apple core of Genesis 3 or the fertile ground of Genesis 1? Do we start with the moment the garden became uninhabitable? Or do we begin with the dirty knees and contented smile of God? The blood of Jesus invites us to begin our story all the way back on the first morning when God called us very good.

In my garden, the flowers are blooming. Just this morning, a hummingbird whipped around the hydrangeas outside my office window, almost crashing into the glass. Perhaps it wanted to break through the screen and join Amy and me for spiritual direction. You could hardly blame it; there was so much sweetness inside.

The hummingbird buzzed as Amy shared about a moment from her church community group. Unprompted, the other women in the room had started giving her feedback. In specific, significant details, they cataloged Amy's gifts and marveled at the way she uniquely reflected God to the world. They named her ground and called her very good.

"It was actually pretty uncomfortable." Amy laughed. "I kept thinking, 'No. That's not real.' Like I couldn't receive it, you know? Like those things couldn't apply to me."

I watched the hummingbird as Amy sighed, a smile pulling at the corner of her mouth. "But I tried to believe them. I chose to tell myself, 'God made me in these specific ways, and that is good.' Since then, God has been so tender to me. Receiving kindness from these women made it easier to receive kindness from God. The other day, I woke up, and do you know what God was saying?"

I shook my head.

"I love you." She beamed. "He woke me up saying, 'I love you.'"

Amy's Creator called her very good, and she—like King David—believed him. If we are brave enough to follow Amy's and David's lead, if we call God's creation (including ourselves) "very good," we see a wonder in our personhood to match the night sky. Constellations of stretch marks and strong muscles tell the story of growing life. Our freckles and folds tell of days in the sun and good, rich food. We touch and smell, dance and scream, sigh and have sex. Our bodies declare the glory of God.

Like our bodies, our inner worlds are a landscape of feelings, preferences, and temperaments. We are moved to tears and have no idea why. Tension knots our stomachs, laughter bubbles out of our mouths, and anger makes us sweat. Our emotions bind us to the world like a web, weaving strands of connection to our own lived experiences.

Our minds take it all in. Gathering data and making observations, we catalog the mysteries of the universe in memory and cognition. We analyze and argue, imagine and consider. Our minds allow us to trace God's movements both beyond and within ourselves.

In a glorious interplay, it all weaves together in a wild act of creation. Body, soul, heart, and mind wrap in the helix of existence and—in the greatest mystery of all—bear the image of the God of the universe. God made us very good. Very good, indeed.

PRACTICE: SPIRITUAL LOCATION

When Lindsey visited our property, she spoke broadly about the land, exploring concepts like soil quality and land erosion. Similarly, many tools for self-knowledge lend themselves to the big picture. Personality assessments like the Enneagram and Myers-Briggs can help us understand our temperaments. Love language assessments and conflict style tests can help us understand how we interact with the world.

While these large-scale resources are useful, sometimes we want to zoom in closer. The Spiritual Location exercise helps us narrow our focus to the present moment.[4] We "name our ground" by examining our current inner landscape in prayer.

The Spiritual Location exercise is a check-in practice that helps us take stock of our lives. It's contemplative and patient. There are six questions to consider, all of which invite curiosity and not criticism. This isn't a test; there are no wrong answers. As we pay attention to our lives, we find God waiting to meet us there. Self-awareness becomes an act of surrender.

1. **Settle.** Take a few deep breaths as you enter prayer. Consider the God of the garden breathing life into

you. Let your breath sync up with his as he says, *Very good*.

2. **Consider.** Ponder the questions below for a few minutes before responding to each in one short sentence. In this season of your life:
   a. What have been your dominant thoughts?
   b. What have been your dominant feelings?
   c. What has been the condition of your body?
   d. What has been your strongest desire?
   e. How are you coming to prayer? Where are you today?
   f. What is God doing *in this season of your life*?
3. **Reflect.** Read over your responses. What's it like to scan your list? End your prayer time talking with God as you would with a friend.

5

THE FLOWER FARM

Naming Desire in Prayer

Go to the limits of your longing.
Rainer Maria Rilke[1]

Just outside of Omaha, where miles of cornfields meet the wide Platte River, there is a sprawling Ignatian retreat center. If you didn't know it was there, you might miss it. One minute, the horizon is nothing but sky; the next, a pair of cast-iron gates open onto a beautifully landscaped complex.

A shuttle waits in the gravel parking lot to take visitors to the Stations of the Cross, a contemplative stroll through Jesus's final hours. Larger-than-life bronze statues line a path through the woods, catching shadows and light from the swaying trees. The final station lets you enter the tomb, where a statue of Christ's dead body lies on a plinth. The last time I visited, a woman was kneeling beside the statue, near the place where Jesus's arm hung limply off the table. She stroked it softly as she cried.

The lodges where the retreatants stay are nestled behind the lake, past the main chapel. Don't let the word "lodges" throw you. There's nothing rustic happening there: think heated bathroom floors and large, open windows. The Cloisters, as it's called, offers free retreat weekends to anyone who wants to step out of the rhythms of daily life and connect to God in the beauty of nature and high-thread-count bedsheets.

With delicious food, spiritual direction, guided services, and silent grounds, The Cloisters brims with the promise of rest. As you might imagine, the waitlist for these retreats is epic. (As of this writing, I'm currently 118th in the queue for a weekend in September.)

So last spring, after three years on the waitlist, I was shocked when an email popped into my inbox saying the wait was over and my spot was secure. I could finally go! But as I cleared my calendar and started planning for the weekend, I noticed something strange. Inexplicably, I kept hoping something would come up and force me to cancel my reservation—maybe a head cold or a forgotten school concert. *Weird*, I thought. *What in the world is this feeling?*

Life in the world of spiritual direction had taught me that when those big emotions pop up—especially if they don't make sense—it was wise to pay attention. Rather than minimizing or dismissing my response, I brought it to prayer.

What I found surprised me. As I am wont to do, I expected my resistance to be the result of some sort of dysfunction. Perhaps I was fearful, hesitant to rearrange my schedule and let other people down. Maybe I was too comfortable, unwilling to give up my cell phone service and BBC cozy murder mystery shows. Tugging on the laces of my spiritual boots, I entered direction with a purpose: repent and get my attitude right.

But Jesus invited me to something different. With a bit of embarrassment, I confessed my reluctance. *Why am I dreading this?* I asked him. *It's my dream weekend.* With his customary patience, he listened as I vented all my concerns. Then, slowly, he helped me interpret myself. It turned out that the root of my tension wasn't the disorder I expected but rather desire. As Ignatius of Loyola would say, it was a call to the *magis*.

Magis is a Latin word meaning "more." In the context of contemplative prayer, it's used to illustrate a sense of deepening. God always invites us to grow in our experience of love, grace, joy, and generosity. *Magis* draws us deeper into God; if God is an ocean, *magis* is the undertow.

With the Spirit as my interpreter, I began to understand my discordant responses. I wanted more. Instead of a shared retreat at The Cloisters, I wanted isolation. Instead of hours dedicated to silence, I craved days in total solitude. *It's okay. You'll be back*, God whispered as I let my reserved spot go, not without regret. *But for right now, have a little less.*

And that's how I found myself at the aptly named Eden House, an Airbnb at a small flower farm in middle-of-nowhere Nebraska, instead of The Cloisters. From the moment I checked myself in through the mobile app to the moment I drove away with a vase of flowers on my passenger seat, I didn't talk to anyone. Unless you count the cat that snuggled up on the patio furniture, I was completely alone. There was never a need to look at the clock. In the long fields of echinacea and phlox, all the world held its breath and time stood still.

Ending up at the flower farm was something of an altar stone for me; it marked a significant moment in my long and complicated relationship with desire. In my early days of flannelgraphs and picture Bibles, I internalized the idea that desire was bad. Perhaps it was never explicitly stated, but I could see the evidence for myself. David. Samson. Eve. You can only tiptoe through a minefield of apple cores, gouged-out eyes, and murdered spouses for so long before growing a bit wary. Desire, it seemed, drove even the most stalwart of believers down the slippery slope to sin. One minute, you feel invincible. The next, the pillars holding up your world are falling around your head.

Desire was the siren song of laziness—the catalyst for all my bad choices. In the morning, it hit the snooze button on my alarm clock set for sunrise prayer. In the evening, it topped off my wine glass and turned on reruns of *Midsomer Murders*. No chores or meaningful conversations tonight. Desire got in the way of all my best intentions. Slowly and subtly, it became my enemy.

Perhaps that's why it was so disorienting when Sherri asked me to befriend it. Tucked into the daily rituals that would accompany me through a nine-month guided journey through the Spiritual Exercises of St. Ignatius was a seemingly innocuous pair of questions.[2]

"Question one," Sherri said. "Each morning as you begin the Exercises, ask yourself, 'How am I coming to prayer?' Don't overthink it. Don't journal about it. Simply notice and, in one sentence, say, 'I am coming to prayer ________.' Fill in the blank."

"Question two," she continued. "Ask yourself, 'What do I desire?' Follow the same pattern that you did for question one. Simply notice and, in one short sentence, say 'I desire ____________.'"

It sounded so simple, so easy. Little did I know it would take the bulk of the next year for me to make peace with those two small words: "I desire."

After Sherri, Augustine of Hippo was next to stir the pot. "The entire life of a good Christian is in fact an exercise of holy desire," he writes, which I found quite rude. "You do not yet see what you long for, but the very act of desiring prepares you, so that when he comes you may see and be utterly satisfied."[3]

Petulantly, I acknowledged there was some truth in what he said. Maybe desire had a good role to play, but paying attention to it still felt like putting on a mohair shirt: itchy and ill-fitting. Despite my reticence, I trusted Sherri, and I was smart enough to know that Augustine was much smarter than me. Thus I was resigned, and I began my journey with the idea of holy desire.

Honestly, it didn't feel great. Paying attention to my longings felt incredibly vulnerable. It turns out that disappointment and desire go hand in hand. Learning to name my desires added grit to my prayers, but it also ached like a hunger pang. "I want my son to be well," I groaned in prayer, with a gut punch of the reality that he was not well. Exposure of longing, even to myself and God, was costly.

Mercifully, the Exercises anticipate this. Perhaps knowing the demands that awareness places on a soul, Ignatius chose to start his journey with a six-week meditation on the love of God. Every morning for forty-two wonderful days, I gnawed on God's love like a dog with a bone. If there is any balm for an unmet desire, it's the deep, salty satisfaction of God's ridiculous affection.

As Augustine promised, there is an upside to awareness. A strange thing began to happen as I paid attention to my desires. Worlds opened up within me. Doors I'd kept shut out of fear or shame swung open, and Jesus appeared. Is it any surprise that he was already there, dwelling in both the brightest rooms and darkest corners of my heart? He had been making himself at home among my desires, airing out the stagnant, shining light on the dark, nurturing the beautiful.

As I explored my desires with Jesus, he invited me to push Pause on self-judgment. Desires are moral neutrals; they simply communicate information. Behind every longing is a trace of a holy echo. Even the most grotesque or vile perversions begin as something good. They need an Interpreter—someone to tear away the distortions and lead us to solid ground.

Does God value right action? Of course. Might I need to repent? Perhaps. Is there biblical truth to speak to myself? Quite likely. But in the language of desire, if I jump too quickly to judgment, I cut the conversation short.

David Benner writes, "Prayer is easily ruined when we make it a project—part of a spiritual self-improvement plan. Rather than pushing yourself forward by resolve, allow God to lead you by desire. The most typical evidence of grace at work within us is not awareness of duty but awareness of desire."[4]

In the Exercises, we practiced naming desire and following it all the way to its root. As a silly example, let's say it's

11:00 at night. I'm in my pajamas, wiping the last crumbs off the kitchen counter, when the cabernet catches my eye. *Oh man, I want some of that right now*, I think, despite knowing it'll ruin my sleep and give me a headache. Now I have a choice. I can (a) pour a glass without thinking, (b) ignore the impulse and go to bed, or (c) pause and look to Jesus with holy curiosity. If I choose option c, my desire can become a catalyst for conversation with God. *I really want this wine, Jesus. Thoughts?*

As I pause at the counter and look at the empty glass, my kitchen becomes a sanctuary.

A conversation with God might lead me to new territory; maybe a desire for a glass of wine has nothing to do with a glass of wine. Perhaps it's rooted in sadness—a longing to soothe the ache after a fight with my son. Perhaps it's rooted in exhaustion—a need for some act that resembles self-care. Perhaps it's rooted in nostalgia—the wish to feel close to my grandmother (notorious for plopping an ice cube in a nice cabernet, much to my horror).

Whatever the root of my desire, Jesus will meet me there—the comforter for my parental sadness, caregiver to my tired body, or keeper of my memories. Could I have selected option a or b? Immediately poured a glass or simply gone to bed? Sure. But think of the parts of Jesus I might have missed by not paying attention. Perhaps this is what John Calvin meant when he said, "Without knowledge of self, there is no knowledge of God."[5] The Spirit has made us God's home; knowing our desires is to know him in them.

With the gift of hindsight, I revisit my flannelgraph and picture Bible memories. New scenes emerge. Moses stands on the mountaintop. Fire and clouds roll around him as he boldly asks God for what he wants: "Show me your glory!" I turn the page and see David dancing like a wild man in front of the ark after begging God for its return. In the next scene, Hannah kneels in the temple, looking drunk, sobbing her greatest desire through murmuring lips.

Then there's Jesus. "I thirst," he says, as he aches from the cross. "I have been earnestly longing to eat this meal with you," he tells the disciples on Passover, beaming. "My Father, if there is any way, get me out of this," he groans in the garden. Desires drip from his face in communion wine and drops of blood.

In a final flannelgraph scene, I hang a new story. I place the figures from Mark 10 on the storyboard one by one. Jesus and the disciples go on first, at the top of the road. Around them is a cast of extras: women with water jars, holy men in priestly vestments, children with baskets, fishermen with mangy dogs. Jesus and the disciples are so surrounded that all you can see is the tops of their heads.

The flannelgraph is now filled with the bustling crowd, and I'm ready to place our final character, a blind beggar named Bartimaeus, in the bottom corner of the storyboard. He is as far from Jesus as he possibly could be. With that, the scene is set and the story begins.

From that edge of the storyboard, a voice rings out: "Jesus, Son of David, have mercy on me!" (v. 47 ESV). There is no way for Bartimaeus to cross the crowded scene and get to Jesus, but he is filled with longing and so he screams, "Jesus!" At this point in the story, I turn the eyebrows of the flannel onlookers down. "Stop that," they scold. "Be quiet!" But to no avail. Again and again, Bartimaeus screams the name of

Jesus until someone reaches through the chaotic scene to say, "Take heart. Get up; he is calling you" (v. 49 ESV).

I peel the crowd away. In my mind's eye, Jesus is kneeling in front of Bartimaeus and asking, "What do you want me to do for you?" (v. 51 ESV).

Here, we need to pause because something radical has happened. I take everything off the board except Jesus, the blind man, and the question: "What do you want?"

None of the flannelgraph onlookers would have asked that question. Everyone knows what the blind guy wants from the Miracle Man, right? But Jesus has a way of asking questions that extend dignity; he doesn't make assumptions or blithely initiate healing. Instead, he draws Bartimaeus into connection, asking him to be brave enough to speak his desire to the God of the universe.

"Please. I want to see."

The story ends. The crowd returns. The blind man weeps through seeing eyes. In the final stage of the scene, I place Jesus at the other end of the road, leaving town. Right behind him, I put Bartimaeus, who concludes the story by following Jesus down the road.

May we be brave enough to do the same. May we offer ourselves the same dignity that Christ extends to Bartimaeus: to name our desires at his feet, to listen to his response, and to follow him freely down the road.

PRACTICE: NAMING DESIRE

In this practice, we explore the story of Bartimaeus, reading the biblical passage slowly and letting it expand in our minds. We enter the crowd. We listen to Bartimaeus's pleas. We watch the compassionate Christ ask, "What do you want me to do for you?" Each snapshot draws us deeper into the narrative, until we, too, are at the feet of Christ. Then, borrowing Bartimaeus's bravery, we consider our own answer to the question Jesus poses.

Sometimes, especially in seasons of pain or grief, our desires are easy to name. Other times, our desires feel nebulous, unavailable to us for any number of reasons. No matter. However you come to prayer, be at peace. God's patient, non-anxious presence invites us to begin the journey of awareness and take all the time we need.

1. **Read.** Move slowly through this story from the Gospel of Mark:

    As Jesus and his disciples, together with a large crowd, were leaving the city, a blind man, Bartimaeus (which means "son of Timaeus"), was

> sitting by the roadside begging. When he heard that it was Jesus of Nazareth, he began to shout, "Jesus, Son of David, have mercy on me!"
>
> Many rebuked him and told him to be quiet, but he shouted all the more, "Son of David, have mercy on me!"
>
> Jesus stopped and said, "Call him."
>
> So they called to the blind man, "Cheer up! On your feet! He's calling you." Throwing his cloak aside, he jumped to his feet and came to Jesus.
>
> "What do you want me to do for you?" Jesus asked him.
>
> The blind man said, "Rabbi, I want to see."
>
> "Go," said Jesus, "your faith has healed you." Immediately he received his sight and followed Jesus along the road. (Mark 10:46–52)

2. **Imagine.** Picture the scene. What does it look like? What time of day is it? Close your eyes. Notice the smells, the sounds, and how the air feels.
3. **Notice Bartimaeus.** He realizes Jesus is nearby. What is his face like? What happens when he begins yelling?
4. **Notice Jesus.** He stops and calls to Bartimaeus. What is his face like? What effect does he have on the scene? On you?
5. **Notice yourself** in the scene. Who are you? Bartimaeus? A disciple? Yourself? Where are you in the scene?
6. **Look.** Observe Jesus as he turns to *you* and asks, "[Your name], what do you want me to do for you?" What's it like to hear that question? How do you respond?

7. **Close.** Complete the two questions. Use them to end your time in prayer.

   I came to prayer ___________.

   I desire ____________.

6

SOBRE MESA

Praying the Word

One cannot think well, love well, sleep well, if one has not dined well.

Virginia Woolf[1]

Welcome to La Salsamenta," Clara said, spreading her arms wide as we entered her outdoor kitchen. "I'm so glad you made it!"

So were we. After a morning spent roaming the busy streets of Barcelona, we were ready to escape the heat and spend the next few hours in the shaded garden of Clara's childhood home. After all the guests arrived and the cava was poured, Clara told us what to expect from the hours to come.

"In today's cooking class, I'll share the secrets of my grandmother's paella recipe," she began. "I'll teach you how to make this traditional dish from start to finish. But before we can cook, we must talk about food and what it means to us here in Catalonia."

A jacaranda blossom floated down and landed in my wine glass as Clara spoke. I looked at the trees and breathed in the soft Mediterranean air. The relaxed atmosphere of Clara's garden was an absolute dream and, honestly, a much-needed change of pace.

As vacationers, we Kauffmans are a bunch of overachievers. We don't really do beach reads or poolside naps; we're more the "Let's set new step records on our Garmin watches" sort of travelers. When we see a place, we see all of it. So our time at La Salsamenta felt like a gift, a quiet moment to slow down, munch on kalamata olives, and steam mussels over an open flame.[2]

"To fully enjoy this meal, it helps to understand how we Catalans contextualize food," Clara continued, dropping a dollop of sofrito in the pan. "When we eat, we create community." The smell of garlic wafted up, and we leaned in to watch it sizzle. Clara grinned at our eager faces. "It is not uncommon that we spend an entire weekend eating together," she said. "Family and friends arrive. Everyone is given a job chopping or stirring. Time passes slowly. We pour wine and have conversations around the outdoor fire. Think of it like an American barbecue. When dinnertime comes, sometimes we are still at the table from lunch! Food is connection. Food creates space for family to be together. That's why we say that the best of life happens *sobre mesa*—'over the table.'"

For the next three hours, we didn't just sample food; we embodied the spirit of life sobre mesa. When we arrived at La Salsamenta, we were a group of strangers, but over the table, we cheered for Michele's seventieth birthday, applauded the newlyweds taking their COVID-postponed honeymoon, and wrapped an arm around Hila when an ambulance wail caused her to jump. "Sorry," she said, as she teared up. "That's the sound we use for the bombing sirens in Tel Aviv."

Thirteen strangers showed up at La Salsamenta, but after three hours of sharing life sobre mesa, we left richly connected.

The paella was everything I wanted it to be, from the crust on the pan to the perfectly dense rice. After posing for pictures with our completed dishes, we feasted at the outdoor table under the warm glow of Edison bulbs. We leaned over each other, refilling wine glasses and holding out forks, insisting, "You have to try this tortilla." Laughter floated across the table, and we ate slowly, telling stories of home and groaning over our favorite bites of food.

This relaxed table was so different from the table I'd been setting of late. Meals in our house had become a hodgepodge of necessity. Our calendar was tight (and, concerningly, so was my waistband). As a result, I reframed my relationship with food. Thanks to our family's busy schedule, it was hard to orchestrate sit-down dinners every night. So to cut down on eating out, I started packing salads in Tupperware and putting almonds in my purse. I signed up for a meal service that delivered diet bars and eating schedules to the door. Our sons—who I swear doubled in height that summer—joined me in thinking about food, but on the opposite end of the spectrum, brainstorming healthy ways to get all the calories and carbohydrates their growing bodies needed. Away from this dreamy vacation, our family's relationship with food had shifted.

Overall, this was good. A healthy, evolving relationship with food requires discipline and attention. I know that food is meant to be functional and nutritious. *But*, I thought as a breeze floated sobre mesa, *it can be beautiful too*. There is a time to strategize about vitamins and strength, and there is a time to pause and let a bright cava sparkle on the tip of your tongue.

Since the time of the prophets, biblical authors have served up the metaphor of food to illustrate spiritual truth. David references honey in Psalm 19, tempting us to salivate over the sweetness of the laws of God. Paul, Peter, and the writer of Hebrews allegorize milk (and its more mature, toothy alternatives), leaving readers hungering for knowledge. Jesus, on the heels of the miraculous feeding of the five thousand in John 6, leans over the table and says to the disciples, "My flesh is real food and my blood is real drink" (v. 55).

If we embrace these metaphors, we find a wealth of goodness on our plates. We taste and see that humankind does not "live by bread alone, but by every word that comes from the mouth of God" (Matt. 4:4 ESV).

Like my relationship with food, my relationship with the Bible has evolved. In the early stages of my faith, I consumed the Word like an eager child filling up on new truths, epic stories, and portraits of Jesus.[3] As I grew, so did my hunger. My *Strong's Concordance* claimed a permanent seat on the nightstand, alongside exegetical commentaries and Charles Ryrie's *Basic Theology*. Like my sprouting sons, I was voracious, filling my mind with every meaty concept or salty defense I could devour.

Then one day my appetite shifted. The hearty meals of Greek and full servings of hermeneutics no longer satisfied me. I pushed the plates away, a little concerned. Instead of forcing down mouthfuls of inductive study, I showed my lack of desire to Jesus. "What's this about?" I asked. Slowly and sweetly, he spread his arms and extended a welcome. *I'm so glad you noticed. Pull up a chair and join me at the table. I have a new place set for you.*

It turns out, I had not lost my taste for the Bible; rather, I was longing to consume it differently. Picking the bones of Scripture clean had strengthened me, but I had forgotten to slow down and enjoy its flavor. Like my son, who eats his entire dinner in three double-fisted bites, I missed the nuance of the meal in front of me. Through my longings, God invited me to take my time, close my eyes, and savor the subtleties of the Word on my tongue.

Is there a time to engage the Bible as sustenance? Of course. Theological discourse and biblical exegesis feed our knowledge of God. The Word is functional and nutritious. *But*, I thought as the Spirit floated sobre mesa, *it can be beautiful too.*

This slow savor of Scripture finds a happy home in the practice of spiritual direction, which approaches the Bible as a banquet. Like Clara, a spiritual director sets a long table and assumes there is time to taste every morsel. The director does not use the Bible to instruct, advise, convict, or encourage the directee (although those things may incidentally happen). Instead, the director creates space to pause with a mouthful of parable or psalm. "Notice the subtleties," they encourage. "Savor the flavor. What does it evoke in you?"

Just as hazelnuts bring out different notes in a Chardonnay than salmon does, one specific moment in time brings out different flavors of Scripture than others do. Perhaps we're grieving like Hila. The salt of our tears might change how the Bible tastes that day. Perhaps we're celebrating like

Michele. The sweetness of our season might highlight different notes of a psalm.

The Bible—this mysterious, breathtaking, bewildering book—is profoundly complex. In spiritual direction, we let it be so. Whatever nuanced emotion or cognitive dissonance arises from our time spent in its pages, we taste the bitter and sweet together.

In contemplative prayer, engaging the Bible is not as much about processing information as it is about connecting with God. Food (even spiritual food) is about connection, as Clara would say. The Holy Spirit invites us to the table, feeds us with the Word, and generously waits for our reaction. Our God is a very good host.

When I arrived at La Salsamenta, I turned off my Garmin and cleared my mind of all other vacation activities. Why? Because I trusted my host. I knew Clara had a great meal planned. All I had to do was grab a chair and follow her lead. Spiritual direction engages the Bible in a similarly relaxed way, trusting that the Host has a fantastic meal planned and that all we have to do is taste and see.

I have sensory memories when I share stories about our time at La Salsamenta: the smell of the garlic we rubbed on our bread, the feeling of squeezing a fresh tomato. Even as I write this, my mouth is watering. Clara sent us home with a recipe so that we knew the mechanics of the meal, but the mechanics are not what's making me salivate. The memory of spice and sweetness of connection are what evoke my emotions. Every time I tell stories of paella, I taste the sweet saffron and laughter all over again.

This same magic happens when we feast on the Word. The riches linger in our memory. One day, you're savoring the story of the prodigal son; the next, you're weeping in church over a reading of Luke 15 because you remember feeling the warmth of the Father's gaze and tasting the salt of the elder brother's rage. You haven't just ingested the Word; you've digested it, and, as Sherri likes to say, the heart does not forget.

It turns out Clara was right. The best of life really does happen sobre mesa.

PRACTICE: LECTIO DIVINA

Lectio Divina is a way to pray through the Scriptures contemplatively. Since the days of the early church, this practice has equipped believers to slow down, soak in the Word, and savor the nearness of God.

Typically, the practice unfolds in four movements, like courses in a meal. After choosing a biblical passage, we read through it slowly (*lectio*), meditate on what captured our attention (*meditatio*), respond to God in prayer (*oratio*), and rest quietly in God's presence (*contemplatio*).

The Carthusian monk Guigo II described it this way: "Reading . . . puts food whole into the mouth, meditation chews it and breaks it up, prayer extracts its flavor, contemplation is the sweetness itself which gladdens and refreshes."[4]

While this practice can be done on your own, the best meals are often shared. Consider practicing with a spiritual director or small group of friends.

1. **Come.** Settle into prayer, knowing God has prepared a place for you at his table. Take a deep breath, close your eyes, and sit in silence for a few moments as you orient your heart to God.

2. **Taste** (*lectio*). Read a short passage of Scripture very slowly without analysis. Simply let the words share space with you.
3. **Chew** (*meditatio*). After a short pause, read the passage again and notice what stands out. Avoid "study"; simply let your thoughts be deep and slow. Linger with the words until you are satisfied.
4. **Digest** (*oratio*). Read the passage again and notice your inner responses. How are your heart, mind, and body responding? Are memories or events from your day coming to mind? Start a conversation with God about what you notice. Listen for his reply.
5. **Savor** (*contemplatio*). After a final reading, become still. The work is done. Let prayer and meditation slip away, and sit quietly with the Spirit for several minutes.

7

BURNING BUSHES EVERYWHERE

Looking for God

What can be seen on earth indicates neither the total absence, nor the manifest presence of divinity, but the presence of a hidden God. Everything bears his stamp.

Blaise Pascal[1]

Space is a rare commodity for a young mother. During the time when my hair smelled like spit-up and my bag was full of Goldfish, I realized I needed an outlet. *Writing*, I thought. *I have always loved writing.* So one evening, when the kids were asleep, I sat down to write—which is to say I started scrolling through Facebook. In the "people you might know" carousel at the bottom of the screen, I saw a vaguely familiar name. "Rachel," I muttered aloud. "Isn't that the poet who writes for *Fathom Mag*?" A few discreet clicks confirmed that—yes, indeed—this was the poet, and she had recently moved to our small town.

Despite feeling silly, I clicked the "add friend" button and quickly typed a message: "Hi Rachel. My name is Laura. Could I buy you a coffee and pick your brain about poetry? Here's my number if you're game."

Happily, Rachel wasn't creeped out by my cyberstalking. We met at Harvest Moon on the town square, sipped almond milk lattes, and immediately struck up a sweet literary friendship. Over our steaming mugs, I explained that I wanted to learn how to write poetry. "I think it will help me craft more concise, impactful prose," I gushed.

Rachel grinned and nodded, indulging my pragmatic slant on the creation of beauty. Then she filled my arms with books: Ted Kooser, Billy Collins, Jane Kenyon, Derrick C. Brown. It was a sneaky move. Poetry, that wily creature, is born not out of structured academia but out of slow, savory attention. When she handed me my first collection of Mary Oliver's poetry, the final nail went into my overintellectualizing coffin. I was smitten. Mary's ability to choose the best words is astounding, but even more remarkable is her ability to pay exquisite, devastating attention to the world.

In her poem "Sometimes," she famously provides instructions for living, but not until she has set the scene. The poem opens by the water, where something dark and earless emerges from a pond. Just as an eerie sense of foreboding sinks in, the scene shifts and we stand in a field of wildflowers as thunderheads roll in and an electrical storm cracks the sky with a cacophony of heat and beauty. With hushed dread, Mary names the presence of God, death, and her heartbreaking melancholy.

Only then does she offer her directive.

"Pay attention," she writes. "Be astonished. Tell about it."[2] Simple words, but they roll through me like a peal of thunder. I look around and notice the catbird on the window ledge, the folds of my rumpled bedsheets, and the broken wind chimes on the floor. What if it all means something wonderful? What if it all means something terrifying?

Her instructions for life could just as easily be called instructions for prayer or instructions for faith. Attention. Astonishment. Response. Her words are trustworthy guides for drawing near to God, and my faith is enriched by the bravery they require.

In another poem, "Yes! No!," Mary Oliver continues her theme of noticing daily miracles. "To pay attention, this is our endless and proper work," she writes.[3] Whether it's happening over almond milk lattes or in spiritual direction, the practice (and it is a practice) of paying attention brings the fuzzy edges of life into sharp relief. Suddenly, the most insignificant things are rife with meaning: a child's shoe, the first snow, a bottle of Lexapro on the bathroom counter. It doesn't matter; fuel for prayer is everywhere.

The smallest details can open to a world of astonishment when they're given space to breathe. The content isn't overly relevant. We could explore innocuous stories about mowing the lawn, scrolling on the phone, turning up the radio, or tucking a child into bed. No matter how mundane, every story is lit with God. When we pay attention to the movements of the Spirit in everyday life, we find a world infused with his presence. As Elizabeth Barrett Browning writes:

> Earth's crammed with heaven,
> And every common bush afire with God,
> But only he who sees takes off his shoes;
> The rest sit round it and pluck blackberries.[4]

There are times when, despite our best efforts to "see," the bushes don't seem to be sparking. There's no placing demands on mystery. Even when we're paying attention, God's presence isn't always easy to detect. On the road to Emmaus, the disciples walked for miles before realizing they were journeying with God. In the garden, Mary wept alone long before seeing her Beloved through tear-filled eyes. In the days of the prophets, Elisha's panicked servant awaited certain death. Only later did he see the hosts of heaven. Unaware, all these people walked on holy ground. Earth is crammed with heaven indeed, but sometimes we can't see the flames.

In my office, directees often lament the silence of God:

"I'm looking for God's presence, but I keep coming up empty."

"Why does God feel far off? I believe in him, but I don't experience the divine at all."

"How can I even know if this faith thing is real? I feel so disconnected."

I hold these statements with no small amount of reverence. To anyone seeking the nearness of God but feeling their prayers bounce off the ceiling, his distance can feel, as Jon Guerra sings, like "an aching unto death."[5] What do you do when you look for God and find only empty space? Sometimes, we do not seek because not finding would be a devastation. When I'm with someone brave enough to give voice to doubt, I take off my shoes. What other response can there be to holy ground?

Last year, in an attempt to get my teenage sons to talk to me, I bought a giant bag of Skittles and an oversized glass jar. Whenever the boys were craving a treat, they could fish out a handful of candy. The only catch? For each Skittle they ate, they had to answer a question about their day. If they pulled a red Skittle, they had to answer a question about something they read or learned. An orange Skittle meant they had to share something awesome; a yellow one, something not so awesome; and a purple one, some classmate or teacher news. But the hardest Skittle of all—the dreaded pull—was green: "Okay, men. Tell me about a kindness shown or received today."

They would roll their eyes in exasperation and insist that with sports rivalries, upshooting testosterone, and demanding schedules, the world of middle school boys wasn't exactly brimming with kindness. But soon enough, the glass jar would be all green, and sugar-lust proved incentive enough to reconsider. Before long, I heard stories of shared pencils, encouraging back-pats, and invitations to the lunch table. Happily, they conceded that kindness had always been there; they simply had to learn to look for it. As they exercised the muscle of attention, they began to see the world through kinder eyes. With the help of neon candies and a little high-fructose corn syrup, my children learned to pay attention to the goodness at their fingertips.

Sometimes, the work of attention requires an ally—someone to offer the Skittle, teach about poetry, or (like Elisha) ask God for a glimpse of the unseen. When my boys were weighed down by the social politics of middle school, they didn't need a lecture on perspective; they needed a listener to believe in kindness and ask good questions. When I consulted Rachel about poetry, I didn't need a primer on structure or form; I needed a friend to draw my attention to beauty. When Elisha's servant was overwhelmed with fear, he didn't need to pull himself up by his spiritual bootstraps; he needed someone to pray for him. Holding belief, inviting attention, and praying for the gifts of revelation: This is the work of an ally. This is the role of a spiritual director.

One of the theological assumptions of spiritual direction is that God is not a far-off, unconcerned Creator who sits back with a bag of popcorn to watch the drama of the world play out. If the incarnation taught us anything, it is that ours is a God who bleeds, who spreads himself on "the road, the rocks, and the weeds."[6] Not content to remain at a distance, he has woven himself into the fabric of every significant and mundane moment. Even now, as you hold this book, he dwells in the ink, curious for your response, whispering from the margins.

His Spirit sets the world alight with burning bushes. Every funeral parlor or graduation stage is infused with the holy. Every bottle of gin or new Mercedes is aflame with the nearness of God. He is constantly calling. Our work is to stand at attention.

There's a story in C. S. Lewis's *The Silver Chair* when Jill and the unfortunately named Eustace wish to journey to Narnia. They decide to call on Aslan (the Christ figure who seems, at that moment, very far away) and ask him to take them there. (Before long, they are whisked into adventure, although not immediately and not as expected.) When they finally see Aslan, he mentions that *he* called *them* into Narnia. Hesitantly, Jill corrects him: Actually, they were the ones who called. Aslan replies that they would not have called unless he had called them first.

Could it be that whenever we direct our attention to God, we're responding to the whispers of the Divine? Perhaps when we seek God, we discover we have already found him.

The bittersweet desire for an experience of God's nearness primes us to receive it. He comes to us even (*especially?*) when we doubt. On the road to Emmaus, Jesus sidled up to the confused disciples in a moment when they presumed his presence was an impossibility. In the garden, Jesus was a quiet witness to Mary's pain when she believed he was dead. In Elisha's courtyard, when enemies were closing in, the terrified servant was only alert to his fear. None of these people sought a holy connection: Their pain and anxiety were far too great.

But God was never far off. Before long, he lets them see. Jesus fell into step with the Emmaus disciples, whispered Mary's name in the dawn, and opened the eyes of the quaking servant. He is always closer than we think.

This call to attention comes again in the story of the burning bush. As far as we know, Moses wasn't seeking a divine encounter the day he met God. He was just watching sheep and going about his everyday business. Then unexpectedly, the bush erupts, the shoes come off, and the great I AM says his name.

In one of the more unremarked upon parts of the story, Moses "saw that though the bush was on fire it did not burn up. So Moses thought, 'I will go over and see . . .'" (Exod. 3:2–3). This reading is so familiar that it is easy to miss the astonishing amount of time contained in those few words. Think about how long it takes for something to "burn up." When we light a brush fire here in Iowa, the smoke is visible for miles. Fallen trees and brown grasses blaze for hours, constantly rekindled by debris and breeze. It's not uncommon for an ordinary controlled burn to last all day. When Moses noticed a fire wasn't going out, it was a miracle of attention. He must have looked at the flames and then—much later—looked again. Considered. Waited. Wondered. Soon, God would speak, miraculously and dramatically commanding Moses to come close. But first, Moses noticed that something was sparking.

When a directee curls up in my leather chair and prayerfully considers their life, I join in the search for what's sparking. Together, we pause, take in the landscape, and say, "It seems like something's burning over there. Let's go over and see." Even if the enemies of depression or addiction are closing in or the daily rhythms of "just watching sheep" feel mundane, we trust that the ground is no less holy for the pain. Sparks of the Spirit rise even when we're unaware.

The call to attention can be soft—a slant of light, an unexpected consolation. It can also be dramatic and wild—a strong voice booming from a bush. And sometimes, it can be both.

On Halloween a few years back, I experienced a call to attention both fierce and still. Blame it on my costume (honoring the Día de los Muertos) or the childlike return to dressing up, but something brought my attention to my grandmother Edna. As I pinned a chrysanthemum in my hair, I blinked against the tears that threatened to undo my face paint.

Six months before, Edna had died after a decade-long battle with Alzheimer's. In my nomadic youth, I had barely known her; when I finally settled down, her mind was not available to be known. Instead, our knowledge of each other was mainly embodied, a language beyond words, a language of hugs and hand-pats, of rocking-chair rhythms and repeated pleasantries, honored not for their content but for the cords they strung between us. When I finally lost Edna completely, I wondered if I'd had her at all.

On that Halloween night a few months later, emotions and grief coalesced at my fingertips. I grabbed my laptop, pulled a stool to the kitchen counter, and began to write. Memories of Edna flashed in my mind: her icy living room (which never soothed the pain from her childhood heat stroke), the constant hum of Atlanta Braves baseball playing in the background, the midnight sandwich she served to a jet-lagged girl (which tasted like nothing if not home). Costumed in my kitchen, I paid attention to the imprint of her life on mine, amazed by the ways she'd shaped and blessed me. As I celebrated and grieved her, poetry poured out in response. Every poem was my act of reclamation. I had lost Edna, but she was not lost to me. I chose to remember, to be astonished. There, among the candy wrappers, my first book of poetry was born.

Looking at the poems I'd created, I felt a spark of the holy and asked, "Can these be my prayers?" Jesus pulled up a stool beside me, collected the poems, and bottled my tears. He came to me, sparking sweetness in the tinder of my pain.

Attention. Astonishment. Response. I hoped Edna, Mary, and Jesus were proud.

PRACTICE: EXAMEN

The examen is a prayer of attention. In this prayer, we reflect on our day with God, recalling moments of light and dark. This practice guides us in tracing the Spirit's movements in our everyday experience.

There are many types of examen: of time (a day, week, or season), of an event (a celebration or a death), even of a virtue (love or hope). The examen below is based on time. It's a good entry point for those who are new to the practice and a great "home base" for those who've been praying the examen for years.

If you're new to the examen, don't worry if it is difficult at first. Building muscle takes time. With each practice, we grow stronger, cultivating an awareness of the presence of God. By building the spiritual muscle of attention, we find a world saturated with Jesus. With the Spirit as our guide, the examen teaches us to seek and find the Lord.

1. **Prepare.** Take a deep breath. Close your eyes. Sit in silence for several minutes as you orient yourself to Jesus's loving presence.
2. **Look back.** Ask the Spirit to guide your memory through your day. Don't work too hard or worry

about remembering every event. Instead, allow scenes from your day to play in your mind like a slideshow.

3. **Look for the light.** Trace the movements of God in your day. When did you notice the fruit of the Spirit: love, joy, peace, patience, kindness, goodness, faithfulness, gentleness, or self-control? When did you notice the spark of his presence?
4. **Look at the dark.** Consider the dark places of your day. When did God feel far off? What wounds did you inflict or receive? What sorrows? Invite God to meet you there. Open yourself to his comfort or forgiveness.
5. **Look ahead.** Consider what lies ahead. What grace do you need from God? Is God extending an invitation to you? Allow him to guide your attention.
6. **Rest.** Take a moment to soak up God's loving gaze. The work is done.

As an alternate examen practice, consider the poem below. Use it as a springboard to write your own liturgy of everyday prayer.

Drishti

My soul was shy
so my body led
the liturgy
of everyday prayer.

Snow fell on the fields
and I looked (a praise)
at ice droplets frozen
in the arc of their fall.

Soapy water
scalded my knuckles
as I scraped (a pardon)
at yolks on the plate.

The puppy came close
and I scratched (a plea)
under her soft
penny-colored ears.

I watered the plants.
I texted a friend.
I drank my cup of coffee
slowly.

Amen, amen, amen.

8

PURE IMAGINATION

The Playfulness of Prayer

> Play is the mediator of the invisible and visible.
>
> Dora M. Kalff[1]

Nancy balanced a paint roller on her hip, wrapped her arm around the rung of a ladder, and snapped a picture from the top of the A-framed church. She texted it to me with a nervous grin and the message that she was "going for it." Behind the ladder and goofy expression, I saw the walls of the church brightening under her care. Nancy, a fellow student at the School for Spiritual Direction, had accepted a position as a children's director at her local church. The first order of business? Fresh paint, all the way up to the gabled roof.

Despite feeling a little wobbly in the knees, I laughed at her text; it was so like my friend to brave the heights, roll up her sleeves, and prepare a place for the kingdom come. A few months earlier, when considering whether to accept the pastoral position, she sensed God appealing to her artistic side. *This place is your canvas*, he said. So perhaps I should have seen this coming. Nothing made more sense than Nancy on a ladder with a big can of Benjamin Moore.

More than anyone I know, Nancy blends the line between "play" and "pray." Recently, she told me about her church's "sacred space," a children's activity created by longtime volunteer Miss Jenny. Kids slip off their shoes, take deep breaths, and enter the prayer room. Their senses come alive as they move freely from station to station—stretching on yoga mats, digging through sand trays, crafting banners for holy seasons, sorting through baskets full of rocks and feathers, and listening to the water feature trickle in the background. There are Bible books and prayer cards in the room too—things more typically associated with spiritual formation—but the real gift of this room is that it allows children to see that prayer is a meeting place, a sensate place where they experience Jesus through the feel of the cross in their hands and the smell of lavender on the altar. In this room, children meet with God in the same way they engage the rest of the world: with play. I imagine Jesus watching them craft and wrestle, read and explore. "The kingdom of heaven?" He says. "It belongs to such as these" (Matt. 19:14).

Nancy's playful prayer isn't limited to children. At a Lenten retreat, she invited the adults of her congregation to creative, hands-on prayer. Running their hands across sandpaper, the participants prayed through the abrasive edges of their lives. Untying knots in a rope, they asked God to loosen kinks in their spirits. The last time I saw Nancy, she brought gel plates, a rubber brayer, and heavy-bodied acrylics so we could pray in colors.

In the wild paradox of our holy, earthy faith, we find that prayer is both a serious and a playful business. At times, prayer is grave: a battleground for deliverance, a pyre for the brokenhearted, a threshing floor for repentance, and a threshold to the presence of the all-consuming God. At other times, prayer is lighthearted and sweet: a parade of song, a palette for the imagination, and a playground for the love of Jesus. Fred Rogers said, "Play is often talked about as if it were a relief from serious learning. But . . . play is serious learning . . . play is the real work."[2] The wisdom of Mister Rogers offers insight into prayer as well. Playing—and its cousin, rest—are not a relief from serious praying; they are serious praying. The one does not diminish the other.

As I write this, I'm in Wichita for a spiritual direction conference, and two little boys have emerged from the house across the street from my Airbnb. One is wearing safety goggles and a Captain America shield, and the other has a bow slung across his shoulders, oversized cowboy boots up to his thighs, and a lightsaber in his fist. Mom and Dad join, and before long, one boy branches away from their family stroll to stand at my porch rail and demand, "And who are YOU?"

I can't help but laugh. The honest unselfconsciousness of children delights me. Madeleine L'Engle writes, "When we can play with the unself-conscious concentration of a child, this is: art: prayer: love."[3]

Watching the children grab their balance bikes and roll away, I envy them. Their self-forgetfulness, candid words, and fearless flamboyance look a lot like holy freedom to me. As they charge into the distance, I wonder what it would look like to show up with my first-draft statements and a curious mind.

From the now-quiet porch swing, my imagination wanders to the biblical story of Jesus and the children in Mark 10. Anachronistically, the little children of Israel wear Spider-Man masks and carry Minecraft swords. The serious crowd of adults reminds me of the mom and dad on the street of my Airbnb—apologizing for their child's blunt words and telling their boys not to disrupt. There is a well-intentioned energy in the parental correction; they want to honor my space and not interrupt whatever important work must be happening as I tippity-tap away on my laptop. Little do they know their blunt babies are brimming with holy energy. As they walk away, I whisper my own version of Jesus's reply to the disciples: "Let those superhero cowboys come to me, and don't forbid them. The kingdom of heaven really does belong to people like them."

In the biblical continuation of this story, Jesus tells the adults that if they want to enter the kingdom, they have to become like little children. The tension of this statement bubbles up in me. Here on this porch swing in Wichita, I'm writing toward my deadline. I'm squeezing in a few hours of work before I head to a series of lectures on the neuroscience, historicity, and cultural implications of prayer. My backpack is so full of books that it takes two hands and consciously bent knees to lift it.

When I get home, my house and family will show the signs that Mom has been gone for three days. In my life, I wear a hundred hats; most days I'm a writer, director, chauffeur, partner, owie kisser, dinner prepper, dirty-sock collector, conflict manager, party planner, avid reader, and Bible studier. But a child? Not often.

Perhaps these young Wichita prophets wheeled by to remind me that I cannot analyze or work my way into the kingdom. I take myself so seriously. Perhaps, in his kindness, Jesus is trying to get me to come and play.

"Let Laura come to me," I hear him say to all my seriousness, "and don't forbid her."

So I close the laptop and retreat to the table, where Nancy has covered the work surface with craft paper and squeeze bottles of paint. Settling onto a kitchen chair, I grab a glue stick and begin to pray.

Much to my surprise, I've found that the playful elements of prayer have fed my soul as much as the serious ones. When I started spiritual direction, I expected to pray in a low, gravelly kind of whisper—maybe nodding my head in reverent silence or grunting little "Mmms" at Sherri's wisdom.

Honestly, I wasn't far off—those things have definitely happened—but what I didn't anticipate was how playful spiritual direction would be. It is unfiltered and charged with full-bodied emotion. "People are always surprised by the laughter," Sherri told me once. "My coworkers will walk by and say, 'Weren't you doing spiritual direction in there? We could hear you guys laughing all the way down the hall!'"

As you might expect, there are endless ways to "play" with prayer. *Visio divina* (like *lectio divina* but with imagery) explores God in beauty. Creative journaling invites us to pray through art. Prayer walking draws us to God in movement. Hymns, both familiar and new, let prayer become a song. All of these are forms of spiritual play: practices for joy and recreation rather than production or a specific purpose.

Margaret Guenther captures the tone of playful prayer beautifully when she writes,

> Play exists for its own sake. Play is for the moment; it is not hurried, even when the pace is fast and timing seems important. When we play, we also celebrate holy uselessness. Like the calf frolicking in the meadow, we need no pretense or excuses. Work is productive; play, in its disinterestedness and self-forgetting, can be fruitful.[4]

Of all the playful prayer practices, my favorite (am I allowed to have a favorite?) is imaginative prayer. It is a hard-won love. For a long time, I thought of imagination as a departure from reality. It was the fanciful, head-in-the-clouds creation of something that didn't exist. Only later did I discover imagination is "the act or power of forming a mental image of something not present to the senses or never before wholly perceived in reality."[5]

Whenever I remember the smell of my grandmother's kitchen, I use my imagination. Whenever I shoot confetti poppers and pull out a spreadsheet for my New Year's resolutions (a Kauffman family obsession), I use my imagination. Every time I pray and orient myself to a Being who is never wholly perceived, I use my imagination. Imagination, it seems, is not a departure from reality but a means of engaging it.

It comes as no surprise to me that Jesus is the master of the imagination. Over and over, the Pharisees come to him with demands of the mind. The law. Rabbinical authority. Death and taxes. Instead of straightforward answers and logical analysis, Jesus often answers with appeals to their imagination. "There was a man who had two sons . . ." (Luke 15:11) or "The kingdom of heaven is like a treasure hidden in a field . . ." (Matt. 13:44) or "I am the true vine, and my Father is the gardener" (John 15:1).

Our logical minds know that what Jesus says here isn't strictly "real." The prodigal son is a fictional character. Heaven isn't lying in some guy's field, and Jesus certainly isn't a leafing plant. But Jesus knows things don't have to be *real* in order to be *true*. Sometimes, the gifts of story, imagination, and metaphor help us wrap our minds around mystery in ways that logic and fact cannot. By appealing to the imagination, Jesus broadens our experience of truth, allowing it to both include and transcend knowledge.

Using stories to stir our imaginations, Jesus communicates wisdom and evokes the senses. Instead of simply reflecting on the lessons of the prodigal, we listen for the sound of pounding feet and feel the warmth of the Father's tears. By using simile, Jesus teaches us about the kingdom of God while also evoking the excitement of a treasure hunt. By using metaphor, Jesus expounds on his oneness with the Father while also letting us touch the pruning arms of the Gardener. Our imaginations in the hands of the Holy Spirit lead to experience as well as information; they lead us to God.

Back in Wichita, as I watch my young friends roll down the road, I'm struck by the irony that writing this chapter has been a lot of work. I approached it like a student, my backpack stuffed with research, data, and practical examples. As I gathered knowledge about the concepts of play, the brain, and prayer, my stacks of books created a mental logjam. The words wouldn't flow. Happily, God sent a couple of caped crusaders to remind me to play, so I decided to ditch my thesis and write a poem.

I'll end this chapter with the silly, imperfect, wild-edged words those young boys inspired. May it be my "amen."

Playing God[6]

If you play God, play God at hopscotch.

Throw all your stones on the ground.
Skip a step or two, sometimes.
Learn to shift your weight.

If you play God, play hide-and-seek.

Hunt for the holy under the stairs.
Search for the sacred behind the door.
Let yourself be found.

If you play God, play God at charades.

Mime your life in gestures and jumps.
Point and flap and screw up your face.
He'll always say the perfect word.

If you play God, play Simon Says.

Listen for his every command.
Follow each word, even when it's strange.
Laugh at the times you get it wrong.

If you play God, play God at tag.

Chase him across the empty lawn.
Slow your step when he's getting close.
Cheer when you snag the hem of his robe.

If you play God, let your play be prayer.

PRACTICE: IMAGINATIVE CONTEMPLATION

Let's play! In this exercise, we enter the world of the Bible, engaging our creative minds and asking the Lord to "sanctify [our] imagination[s] and help [us] experience the real Jesus 'with all five senses.'"[7] Using a Gospel story as a springboard, we envision the scene, exploring the narrative's richness in new ways.

Some of us are imaginative by nature, and practices like this will probably come easily. But if your temperament doesn't lend itself to creativity or imagery, don't worry: God is pleased that you're engaging his Word, regardless of your imaginative "success."

As you practice exploring the Word with all five senses, keep in mind that a sanctified imagination will always bear the fruit of the Spirit and align with the Word. If it feels like that is not happening, simply open your eyes, take a deep breath, and realign with who you know God to be.

If you are new to imaginative prayer, a spiritual director or a prayer partner can be especially helpful. However you practice, take heart. The Spirit is a good guide, and his sheep know his voice. He is more than able to guide you into a deep, faithful, felt experience of his Word.

1. **Prepare.** Choose a Gospel story for your reading (such as the story of Zacchaeus from Luke 19:1–10 or the healing at the pool of Bethesda from John 5:1–9).
2. **Pray.** Ask God to sanctify your imagination and help you experience the real Jesus with all five senses.
3. **Rest.** Take a quiet moment before you begin. Breathe. When you are ready, read the passage slowly.
4. **Imagine the setting.** Use the questions below to engage your senses. For this practice, don't worry too much about historically accurate context (like clothes or architecture). Instead, imagine:
   a. The sights. What's the setting like? Consider the landscape, the time of day, the crowds.
   b. The sounds. Are there birds? The bustle of a crowd? Dogs? Notice what sounds come to mind.
   c. The atmosphere. What does the setting feel like? Hot? Cold? How does the air smell?
5. **Imagine the scene.**
   a. Where is Jesus? The disciples? Imagine the characters of the scene, from their clothes to their expressions.
   b. What action takes place? Watch the story play out in your mind's eye.
   c. Place yourself in the scene. Where are you? Who are you?

6. **Go to Jesus.** Imagine Jesus drawing near to you. How do the two of you interact? Close your prayer by soaking up the graces of meditating on this Gospel story.

9

FLESH AND BONE

The Physicality of Prayer

> I will make the poems of my body and mortality,
> For I think I shall then supply myself with the
> poems of my soul and of immortality.
>
> Walt Whitman[1]

Not too long ago, I watched as my oldest son grabbed a fishing pole, revved up an outboard motor, and puttered to the remote edges of the lake. Standing on the shoreline, I could see his silhouette as he maneuvered through the water. By age fifteen, he already had at least six inches on me, and had become the one we called for anytime we needed some heavy lifting done. When I watched his strong arms shove the boat away from the shore, I marveled at the miracle of his body.

Caleb has his father's olive skin and the Crabtree family nose. His hands are etched with veins from hours spent at the piano, and his legs bear crosshatched scars from a recent bout with poison ivy. Along his back, from the nape of his neck to his waistband, is a long, jagged scar, the remnant of a series of surgeries that rebuilt his spine. The scar is almost as old as he is. It stretches with his growing torso, curving around his muscles and bending with his newly diagnosed scoliosis.

He wears his story on his skin. His broad shoulders show evidence of hours in the high school gym in fierce competition with his lifting buddies. His sleeplessness goes back to his second surgery; the night terrors have ended, but he still can't make peace with the dark. His body is strong and vulnerable, resilient and scarred. When I was pregnant with him, a doctor told me there was a brain anomaly in his routine prenatal scan that might take his life minutes after birth. Later, in the bright delivery room, when the nurse placed his tiny body on my chest, he was warm, whole, and alive. We counted ten perfect fingers, ten perfect toes, and two lungs that could rival a bullhorn. We named him Caleb. *Faithful*.

From the moment he was born, I was lost to the immediate mercy of his body in my arms. I marveled at every bit of him: the clean smell of his head, the fuzz on his downy cheeks, the startling clarity of his eyes. Every moment he wasn't in my arms was agony; I wanted the weight of him in the crook of my elbow and the soft sighs of his breath on my shoulder.

Whenever his body communicated (which it did a *lot*), we listened. We loved the way his body spoke for him. Every contented sigh or colicky scream echoed with the miracle that he was alive.

Look at him, God whispered to me years later. *Remember when he was a baby? How his tiny body filled you with joy? Look at him now.* I grinned. *Delighted, right?* He continued, *And* that *is how I feel about* your *body. Your physical, human, flesh-and-blood body brings me that kind of joy.*

It's a beautiful sentiment, the thought that my flabby thighs, creaky knees, and green eyes delight the heart of God. Looking at my son, I can almost believe it. But my body and I have a complicated relationship; for too many years, I have appreciated and critiqued it, used and misused it, loved and hated it. An unbiased view of my own body eludes me. I have, quite literally, too much skin in the game. If I'm going to see myself with kinder eyes, I'm going to need the gaze of a Parent.

Talk about my kids' bodies, and I have a different set of baseline assumptions than when I think about my own. When the boys snore, sweat, laugh, and run, do I think their bodies are good? Of course. When they groan with pain, spike fevers, or growl with hunger, do I think their bodies are communicating helpful information? One hundred percent. When they snuggle up on the couch at the end of a long day and wrap their now giant arms around me, do their bodies help them connect with me? Without a doubt. As a mom, it is easy to say that my boys' growing bodies are very good, even when they're not perfect.

When I'm brave, I try to lay this parental lens over myself. What if my body is a friend? What if my body's signals (especially about the care it needs) are a blessing and not a distraction? What if—at the end of a long, hard day—my body helps me connect with God?

Watching my son across the lake, I was struck by the stories our bodies tell. Caleb's nose links him to a long line of

Southern itinerant farmers. My middle son, Lucas, is covered in freckles from his many hours spent running with the cross-country team. My fair complexion ties me to a seaside village in Norway.

Across Lucas's freckled forehead is a small, permanent dent—the remnant of the time he plunged headfirst into a wooden steamer trunk. My youngest son, Micah, famous for his easy smile, has a scar running perpendicular to his lip from an accident with landscape timbers. As always, the beautiful shares a canvas with the broken. Our bodies tell the stories of our wounds and the wounds of those who've gone before us.

In spiritual direction, I have witnessed the embodied stories of people who have endured chronic pain, battled mental illness, and survived childhood abuse. Their stories are inscribed on their skin. They wear their history as they stand before God in prayer.

God uses everything for divine connection, including the body, but for those of us who carry trauma, involving the body in prayer can feel risky at best and violating at worst. As psychiatrist and researcher Bessel van der Kolk writes,

> traumatized people chronically feel unsafe inside their bodies. . . . Their bodies are constantly bombarded by visceral warning signs, and, in an attempt to control these processes, they often become expert at ignoring their gut feelings and in numbing awareness of what is played out inside. They learn to hide from their selves.[2]

Trauma teaches us to hide and thus requires a tender hand. After a recent surgery, Caleb was ensconced on the couch with a box of Cheez-Its and an X-box controller. I tried to get him up and moving, but he was tired and perhaps a bit defeated. I knew he couldn't stay on the couch forever. His healing journey had to involve rehabilitation exercises and physical challenges. But as he sat on the couch in the throes of fresh recovery, I also knew I couldn't swoop in on him with an aggressive healing agenda. It would have risked damaging his already wounded spirit.

The same is true for prayer. When I bring myself to prayer, I bring the wounded and weary along with the resilient and strong. If I rush upon the vulnerable parts of my spirit with demands for healing, I risk causing greater damage to myself. God can bring healing we never imagined, but he never bullies us down the road to health. He is a patient Physician.

For this chapter, I hope we can borrow his patience. Reading about the body's interaction in prayer might be troubling for some of us. Take this paragraph as your permission to read slowly and exercise consent, agency, and option.[3] In this chapter, if I ask you to notice your body or its cues, please know that you can ignore the invitation without guilt or shame (consent). Anytime you notice a strong inner reaction to the chapter's content, pause. Set the book down, make a cup of tea, take a beat. Feel free to honor your inner response and act in a way that feels healthful (agency). Finally, if I outline an embodied prayer practice, I will provide modifiers so that meeting God in prayer feels honoring both to your body and to the One who made it (option). All of you, dear reader, is welcome here.

Every Sunday morning, around the world, friends of Jesus hit their alarm clocks, brush their teeth, fight with their children to get out the door on time (a universal truth), and meet at their local churches. This is a challenging season for the American church. Every healing journey begins with a diagnosis, and the church is naming the infections of nationalism, sexism, abuse, and powermongering. This process is both painful and hopeful. God loves his bride too much to let toxic disease lead to death. His kindness is injecting the church body with repentance, but fighting the infection hurts like hell.

Whatever her faults and flaws, the church still pulses with beauty: the holy mystery of the word read aloud, the yeasty warmth of the Eucharist, the humility of the liturgy, and—of course—the singing. "We are one in the Spirit. We are one in the Lord," we sing from hymnals and projection screens.[4] As we sing, we inhale and exhale together. In a physical mystery of connection, our breath syncs up, and research shows our heartbeats do as well.[5] The Republicans and the Democrats, the rich and the poor, the Black and the White, the old and the young, the liberal and the conservative join voices in a unified love song to God. For that moment, we share one heartbeat, and we "pray that all unity will one day be restored." For four beautiful verses, our bodies corporealize what our minds still struggle to grasp.

Not long ago, I experienced this phenomenon during a seminar on embodied prayer. Dr. Rebecca Letterman, a seminary professor and embodiment coach, taught about meeting God in the body. I scribbled notes all over the PowerPoint handouts until my hand cramped in my attempt to capture every word. "Simple movements in prayer can help us create new neural pathways," I wrote. "Prayer postures invite Jesus to teach our bodies (and not just our minds) about holiness." I was still writing furiously when Rebecca clapped her hands and said, "So! Enough talking. Let's practice!"

Awkwardly, we pushed back our chairs and stood up, ready to try a few embodied prayer practices. We grinned nervously at each other as we followed Rebecca's instructions, stretching our arms and clenching our fists.

We began with a star pose, a stretching posture. As we shifted around the room to find space, Rebecca asked us to consider where God might want us to be expansive. "Where do you want me to show up bravely?" I prayed as I stretched my arms out wide. "Where should I take up space?"

"Well," Rebecca said, as we finished. "How was that for you?" The room erupted with positive reports. "I felt so engaged!" "It was so nice to stand before God like that." "It was like raising your hands in worship." Looking at the cheery faces and nodding heads, I slipped my hand up reluctantly. "Umm . . . I hated it," I said, blushing. "I felt so exposed. I was checking for pit stains and worried my shirt was riding up. I wanted to like it, but I felt really . . . vulnerable."

"Yes! That is such good information!" Rebecca affirmed. "And so natural. When our bodies respond, whether it's refreshing or uncomfortable, we learn about what is happening inside us. It becomes a catalyst for even deeper prayer."

After our discussion, we tried another activity: a care posture. Following Rebecca's lead, I reached my dominant hand across my body and placed it on my ribs. My nondominant hand followed suit, crossing to rest softly on my opposite shoulder. I was all bound up in a strange sort of hug as I tilted my head to the side and breathed.

"Jesus," Rebecca prayed. "Meet us in this posture of care. Help us to receive your peace." Wrapped up like little pretzels, we sat there without words and let our bodies pray for us.

It wasn't long before I needed that posture again. Before the seminar, I'd had a political discussion with someone I love and respect. It did not go well. It was fine, I guess, as these things go. There weren't shouts or swears or any of the "first round" sins, but I was unsettled. My defenses popped up far too quickly; I hadn't listened well. So after I got home from the seminar, I apologized, and we tried the conversation again.

As we chatted, my body—that great communicator—began to react. Thanks to Rebecca, the art of interoception was fresh on my mind. *Interoception*, or the awareness of your body's inner cues, revealed that I was gearing up for a fight. I noticed a tight, tingling sensation in my chest and jittery energy in my hands. There is a time to harness holy indignation and use it for good, especially when it spurs us to the work of justice. But my body alerted me that I was about to unleash a torrent of "righteous anger" on someone with whom I was trying to build a connection. This was not the time and place for outrage; thank God my body warned me.

Remembering the seminar lessons, I subtly stretched my hand to my ribs and tilted my head. It's called a "micropose," but the result was large indeed. My body remembered the hours spent in bound-up prayer. I felt the weight of my hand on my ribs, just as I had at the conference. It grounded me. I breathed deeply, tapping into the neural pathways Jesus and I had built together. From that place, God guided me into a more patient, less reactive conversation. My body led me to the fruit of the Spirit when my mind could not.

In the first century, the philosophy of Gnosticism posited the idea that the body was evil and the spirit was good. The body seemed to be nothing but a vessel of sin and death, with all its lusts and violence and base desires. Who could hope to live the holy life when plagued by the demands of the flesh? "No one," the Gnostics concluded, and tried to divorce their souls from their bodies. They sought to rise above the temporal and exist in purely spiritual form as what James K. A. Smith called "brains-on-a-stick."[6]

Some days, that doesn't sound terrible. When illness attacks my body, I would love to transcend it. I hate the demands of pain, the way the fog in my head never clears and my body screams against my will. On other days, when I relive the violence that I have done and that has been done to me, adrenaline obscures my vision. My nervous system pulses on high alert. My face flushes with shame. In those vulnerable moments, the soft light of Gnosticism beckons, and I am tempted by its promises.

On those days, I cling extra tightly to the scarred hands of Jesus. His physical body becomes my consolation. If he does not despise the heartbeats, hormones, and hiccups of the human experience, I don't want to either.

The delivery room continues to grant me gentle access to the body, but this time, I visit a different delivery room. This one is covered with hay and donkey droppings. A teenage girl counts ten perfect fingers, ten perfect toes, and two lungs that could rival a bullhorn. "We'll name him Jesus," she whispers. "God saves."

Did she marvel at the miracle of the Commander of Angel Armies nuzzling her chest? Did she breathe the clean smell of his head, crave the weight of his small body in the crook of her elbow? Did a breeze blow through the stable, making baby Jesus shiver?

As he grew, Jesus learned to walk, entered puberty, and got splinters at his father's workbench. He rubbed mud on a blind man's eyes, touched a leper, and smelled the anointing oils dripping from his hair. In the most horrific and holy act of vulnerability, he let his body be undone. Did he scream when the nails went in? Weep when he gave his mother a new son? From the top of his head to the soles of his feet, his body told the story of his suffering.

Then came the morning. Deep in the tomb, Jesus lay broken in the dark. Everything was cold and still until, out of the heavy silence of death, the body of God started to *breathe*. Rising and falling. Inhaling and exhaling. His scarred hands reached up in the dark, peeled the death cloths away from his face. I wonder what it felt like, sitting there in the dark, covered in oil and wounds, holding cool linen. Did a breeze blow when the stone moved, making the risen Jesus shiver?

In the resurrection, his body told his story; his friends didn't know who he was until they saw the scars. The perfect, holy, resurrected body of God has scars. Once again, he ate fish, built fires, and rested with the disciples until he went home to the Father. His human body—from his big toes to his armpits, from his lips to his fingernails—ascended to heaven. Now, dwelling in the Godhead, is a human form bearing the scents of earth, the scars on skin, and the sound of laughter. A Body lives in the Godhead, and God lives in our bodies. Heaven and earth, flesh and spirit; "we are one in the Lord," indeed.

PRACTICE: BODY SCAN

This exercise invites the body to enter prayer softly. Some versions of the body scan help us detect our inner cues, and other versions help us interact with our pain. We'll leave those more focused practices for another day. In this iteration of a body scan practice, we will simply ask God to give us a physical sense of his love.

As mentioned before, if you notice any physical or psychological discomfort, please stop. Take a break from the practice entirely or start smaller. Rather than scanning your whole body, you might start with a small, innocuous part like a big toe or an earlobe. If that still feels uncomfortable, you might pay attention to what you sense in the room (smells, sounds, etc.). This is a practice of *exteroception* (an awareness of what's around your body) and might be useful if looking inward feels too vulnerable.

If you want extra support, find a Rebecca or a Sherri. A spiritual director is a wonderful resource for guidance, discernment, and care as you engage your body.

1. **Relax.** Find a comfortable posture, lying down or seated in a chair. Take a few intentional deep breaths. Become aware that God is with you.

2. **Anchor.** Close your eyes or invite a soft focus by looking past the tip of your nose. Notice where your body touches the floor or the chair. Grow heavy and relaxed. Sink into the present moment with God and your body.
3. **Invite.** Ask God to guide your attention, then settle into his presence by saying his name in rhythm with your breath or repeating the practice of sitting in his loving gaze.
4. **Attend.** When you feel ready, direct your attention to your feet. Pause. Notice any sensations (tingling, warmth, tension, pressure) that arise. Do not judge or adjust; simply notice.
5. **Imagine.** God is looking at your physical form right now. Some people like to picture God's gaze as a beam of light resting on their feet.
6. **Move.** When you are ready, let your attention move upward. Be aware of the warm light of God's love resting on . . .
    a. Your shins, knees, and thighs
    b. Your hips, waist, lower back
    c. Your stomach, chest, shoulders
    d. Your arms, wrists, fingers
    e. Your neck, jaw, face
    f. The top of your head
7. **Breathe.** Take a few deep breaths, noticing what it feels like to be one complete, integrated being.
8. **Notice.** What did you notice in this practice? Is there a simple, one-sentence response you would like to offer to God?

9. **Begin to invite movement** back into your body, wiggling your fingers and toes. Bless the practice by offering a closing prayer such as, "I praise you because I am fearfully and wonderfully made" (Ps. 139:14).

10

HOLDING HISTORY

Standing on the Shoulders of the Saints

Every man is a quotation from all his ancestors.

Ralph Waldo Emerson[1]

For a brief season in our early marriage, Chris and I were antique pickers. Every weekend, we'd grab a cup of gas station coffee, crank up the classic rock radio station, and lay the newspaper on the dashboard. The classified section was our map, leading us through our city's back roads from one garage sale to another in search of forgotten treasures to sell in our Etsy shop.

We followed countless yard signs around town, in search of a detached garage or a hoarder's barn. If we saw pack-n-plays or power tools in the driveway, we would keep on driving. But if we found an "estate sale" sign with shaky lettering or an old man smoking a pipe under a tree, we'd pull to the curb and stuff dollar bills into our pockets.

Sometimes we'd hit the jackpot. Milk pails and coffee grinders promised a good haul. "Can we start a pile by the cash box?" we'd ask. There's a certain excitement that comes from a treasure trove like that, but my favorite stops were those that required a little more work. Give me a dilapidated barn with water-logged boxes over an organized display table every time. My tetanus shot is up to date; I'm climbing to the hay loft.

At home, we'd scour our newly discovered gems for markings, such as a US Army stamp on a metal canteen or a serial number on a Kodak camera. Research became our second treasure hunt. Google would disappoint us at times, proving we'd grabbed a replica with no real value. But every now and then, our ordinary items would turn out to have historical interest. My favorites were a wooden chair from a telegraph office, a psychedelic light-up sign by Peter Max, and a rare typewriter with lift-up keys.

After exploring the item's history, we'd roll up our sleeves to polish clockworks and wash away decades of dust. As our hobby (*addiction?*) grew, a rhythm developed: snap a photo, list the item, box it up, and sell the treasure. We made just enough money at the end of the day to refill our gas station coffee and reach for the classifieds again.

In between "snap" and "sell," we "stored." Adjustable shelving filled every wall in the basement, the garage, and, eventually, a nearby storage unit. Walking through those rooms felt otherworldly. The scent of old books hung heavy in the air. "If heaven has a smell," I told Chris, "this is it."

Perusing our storage unit felt surreal, like journeying back in time. I would pull an antique from the shelf and turn it over in my hands, almost reverently, imagining the lives of the people who had owned it before. Handwritten epitaphs and sepia photos seemed to cast a haze over what I knew, like heat lines coming off asphalt. The world was familiar but not familiar. Recognizable but mysterious.

It was good to hold a thing with history.

Years later, we've abandoned the rituals of classic rock and gas station coffee, trading them for soccer practices and piano concerts. But deep in the basement, behind the Nerf guns and golf bags, there's a shelf of antiques we can't bear to sell. The lure of history is hard to shake off; I still swerve when I see an estate sale sign.

Sometimes the boys roll their eyes at my secondhand energy. They'll wear a thrift shop Nike sweatshirt, but they draw the line at boxers (even though they still had tags!). My love of the old might lead to some quarrels, but every now and then, I catch them sneaking into the basement to pull something old off the shelf. A typewriter. A BB gun. A World War II insignia.

On a family trip to England, Lucas and Micah ditched the souvenir shop with its latest fads and shiny trinkets for an ivy-covered antique store in the Cotswolds. They shopped in hushed reverence before spending their hard-earned money on a collection of metal RAF soldiers. Don't get me wrong; they still love the shine of something new (you should hear Lucas talk about the latest running shoes), but they've discovered the magic of time, and every now and then, they want to hold a thing with history.

Not long ago, the lure of time reached out for me again. It all started with a question: "Who is it that you seek?" The line from an old prayer, read by our professor, Winn, echoed around the room. We students sat in a circle, bright-eyed and eager for the first day of seminary classes in the "Sacred Art of Writing" doctoral program. Our laptops were closed, and our heads were bent over the printed prayer we found placed at every seat. Holding up the crisp white sheets, we responded as one:

"We seek the Lord our God."

My voice caught with unexpected emotion, and I glanced around the room at the strangers whom I would soon grow to love. There were pastors and priests, writers and spiritual directors from all around the continent, representing a diverse collection of faith communities. Within the walls of the seminary, we were united by the love of God and a passion for the written word.

> "Do you seek God with all your heart?"
> "*Amen, Lord, have mercy.*"
> "Do you seek God with all your soul?"
> "*Amen, Lord, have mercy.*"
> "Do you seek God with all your mind?"
> "*Amen, Lord, have mercy.*"
> "Do you seek God with all your strength?"
> "*Amen, Christ, have mercy.*"

The last repetition made me blush; I had closed my eyes and was caught off guard by the change from *Lord* to *Christ*. Loudly, I (alone) asked the Lord for mercy.

Our handout was entitled "Morning Prayers," and a footnote explained that the words were adapted from the Northumbria Community and *The Book of Common Prayer*. Taking a mental scan of the last decade, I realized this was the first time in years I'd collectively read liturgical prayers.

In my nomadic life, I've worshiped in countless churches and faith communities, but for the most part, they were all in a similar stream: conservative, evangelical, low-church. The services were typically informal and creative, constructed each week around a pastorally selected passage of Scripture.

The only ancient words I encountered growing up (besides the Bible) were sung from the pages of old Baptist hymnals: "Take my life and let it be consecrated, Lord, to Thee." No matter where my roaming feet landed, there was a sense of home when the piano swelled with those opening notes to an old, familiar song. "Take my feet and let them move at the impulse of Thy love."[2]

Years later, in my ecumenical seminary class, I recognized a similar emotion. When the words from *The Book of Common Prayer* were read aloud, they, too, started to feel like home. Every morning before class, we bent our heads and read aloud, like a song. I found myself looking forward to my favorite parts: "Christ under me; Christ over me; / Christ beside me, on my left and my right," and "This day be within and without me, lowly and meek, yet all-powerful."[3]

After we read the prayers, a classmate would share an Epistle and a Gospel passage before we all recited the Lord's Prayer. One day we read all the way from "Our Father, who art in heaven" to "for thine is the kingdom" in about five seconds flat. The next day, our professor, John, asked us to give the reading a bit more time. "We're all in a race to the power and the glory," he said. "Let's see if we can slow it down a bit." After each phrase, we paused, just a little, to let the words breathe.

My tears came unbidden again. *Is it the voices?* I wondered. *The sound of everyone praying together?*

The musicality of the prayer could undoubtedly make a girl misty, but I could just as easily blame the history. For generations, these prayers have echoed through congregations in wooden pews, parishes in quiet countrysides, and cathedrals in bustling cities. Believers across time have recited these exact words; I could almost feel the light from their stained-glass windows shining through the years to bless our seminary classroom.

The heirlooms of faith—old hymns, ancient prayers, common creeds—bear the patina of time. For hundreds of years, believers held these words on their lips and in their hands. They've been worn by use until they shine with the wisdom of generations. My faith—which is necessarily so personal and intimate—grows large and more expansive when woven into a tapestry that predates me and will outlive me. I am my own, and I am not my own. Christ belongs to me, and Christ belongs to us. Holding the prayers of the saints like an inheritance, I borrow the faith of the family of God.

Don't get me wrong. I still love a shiny new spiritual practice or a spontaneous prayer. If you think my kids bring excitement to a conversation about running shoes, you should see me talk about Douglas McKelvey's collections of modern liturgies. Contemporary prayers shine with the character of a new generation. By crafting our unique love song, we add our voices to those who went before us, and I wholeheartedly celebrate that creative energy for the church.

And also. It is good to hold a thing with history.

On one of our garage-sale trips, I found a powder-blue cardboard box tucked among a stack of vinyl records. When I pulled its lid off, I expected to see a collection of LPs but was surprised to find a paper-thin glass plate. The sun caught the gold edges of the Hebrew characters and their English translations, marking the place for the *karpas* (vegetable), *beitzah* (egg), and *chazaret* (bitter herb).

This Seder plate would never make it to our online store. Instead of adding it to the pile of antiques to be photographed, I stored it in our Tupperware box of Easter decorations. Now, every year, when the tulips push up through the mulch, I dig out the powder-blue box again. I lift the glass, wipe away a year's worth of dust from the surface, and prepare to celebrate the Seder.

Ever since the boys were small, we've celebrated the Passover dinner. On the Thursday before Easter—when Jesus would have celebrated his final Passover—we gather at our friends' house just before sunset. The kitchen is transformed. Gone are the barstools and trash pails. Instead, the floor is covered in a vintage tablecloth and the fancy dishes are laid out. We light candles, pour wine, and read from juice-stained Seder scripts (*Haggadahs*).

Our Haggadah is modern and Christ-centric, but the elements of this practice follow the ancient rhythms. We drink four cups of wine (or grape juice), each representing a Mosaic promise. We retell the Exodus story of the plagues and deliverance, complete with flyswatters and Band-Aids for props. (I asked Lucas if we should abandon these childish extras now that he's a teenager. "No way," he scoffed. "Those are the best parts. Some things you just don't outgrow.")

The children around the Seder table tower over me now, but I remember when they were in high chairs, waving their pointer fingers to "This Little Light of Mine." This Seder ritual holds elements of their stories—and not just theirs, but the stories of generations. It holds the unwritten stories of Jesus, a Jewish boy who would have celebrated this meal every year of his life, from his childhood table to the Upper Room. Looking at the kids around my Seder table, I imagine a young Jesus next to them searching for the hidden bread, screaming out the door for Elijah, and laughing at the weird looks they get from the neighbors.

In the middle of the Seder dinner, we read the Dayenu prayer. The Dayenu is a retelling of the exodus, a call-and-response prayer that echoes around the kitchen where we sit on the floor with throw pillows and grape juice. The kids hold their breath between responses, turning red as they wait for their cue to scream their prayers to the sky.

Leader: "If the Lord God had only taken us out of Egypt . . ." (*long pause to see if the children pass out*)

Kids: "IT WOULD HAVE BEEN ENOUGH!" (screamed with heads thrown back, spittle flying)

Leader: "If the Lord God had only taken us out of Egypt and not parted the sea . . ."

Kids: "IT WOULD HAVE BEEN ENOUGH!"

Leader: "If the Lord God had only parted the sea and not given us manna . . ."

Kids: "IT WOULD HAVE BEEN ENOUGH!"

By the end of the prayer, we're all laughing (even though our ears are ringing). The Dayenu goes on and on, chronicling God's extravagant mercies: Sabbath rest, the law, a place to call home. One of these gifts alone would have been enough, yet God shows up with ridiculous, generous abundance.

A few years ago, I pulled this Dayenu prayer down from the shelf, desperate to hold a thing with history. It wasn't the right season for the Passover meal; we were deep in a brutal winter that brought job loss, broken relationships, and cancer scares. But I had seen the gold-rimmed edges of God's kindness and wanted to set the table for remembrance. I longed to polish the dust off my neglected spirit. Gratitude doesn't always start with warm emotion, so I entered with grit. Since my own language was unavailable, I borrowed the form of the Dayenu.

"If God had only made the surgery successful, it would have been enough," I wrote.

"If God had only made the surgery successful and not made me cancer-free, it would have been enough."

"If God had only made me cancer-free and not provided us a job, it would have been enough."

On and on I went, recounting God's mercies. I wasn't in a wild rapture of thanksgiving; I was fighting for praise tooth and nail. My bloodied prayers joined the songs of generations who stumbled through their own winters and deserts. Together, we name our sorrows and mercies, chronicling the faithfulness of God through all generations.

PRACTICE: BORROWING LANGUAGE

In this practice, we hold a prayer with history, borrowing the language and wisdom of the family of God. This exercise is especially helpful in times of transition, seasons of desolation, and rhythms of routine. The words become support beams, offering timeworn treasures to our conversation with the Lord.

While the format of this exercise can be used with any set prayer, this specific reflection will explore the Suscipe from Ignatius's Spiritual Exercises, originally published in 1548.[4] Hundreds of years after its publication, this prayer of surrender serves as a wise teacher and faithful companion.

1. **Pause.** Get settled. Take several deep breaths. Let your mind, body, and spirit sync up. God is with you. Gather an awareness of his love.
2. **Read** your prayer out loud when you are ready. See how slowly you can go.

    Suscipe

    Take, Lord, and receive
    all my liberty,
    my memory,

my understanding,
and my entire will,
all that I have and possess.

Thou hast given all to me.
To Thee, O Lord, I return it.
All is Thine; dispose of it
wholly according to Thy will.

Give me Thy love and Thy grace,
for this is sufficient for me.[5]

3. **Breathe.** Let the words linger. Take a minute of silence.
4. **Read** the prayer again, this time in your head. Go slowly. Pause and repeat any lines that feel meaningful.
5. **Notice** how it felt to pray Ignatius's prayer.
   a. How does your body feel? (pause to notice)
   b. Is there a word or phrase you want to carry with you? (pause to notice)
   c. How does your spirit want to respond to God? (pause to notice)
6. **Jot** down any response on a notecard and leave it somewhere visible. Return to the words anytime you need.

11

PRAYING IN THE DARK

Lament

Where there is sorrow there is holy ground.

Oscar Wilde[1]

It was wintertime. All around, the world was celebrating. The town square looked like a scene from a Norman Rockwell painting: Twinkling garlands wrapped around cast-iron lampposts, snow dusted the cobblestone streets, and the twenty-foot pine tree outside the courthouse boasted a cheery star. The radio stations had shelved their usual playlists to make room for the Christmas classics. Bing Crosby and "Jingle Bells" blasted from every speaker. After cranking up the defroster in my car, I clicked the radio off.

It's a strange thing to hold a profound sorrow while the world is turning up the volume on joy. "We Wish You a Merry Christmas!" "It's the Most Wonderful Time of the Year!"

"Joy to the World!" The holly jolly notes of the season repeated ad nauseam, keeping time with my pounding head. In my chilly car, the silence was a relief.

As the windshield cleared, I watched the snow weigh down the branches of the courthouse pine. A few days ago, a sheet of ice followed a snowstorm and cemented a blanket of white to every fencepost and tree branch. I nodded at the pine in commiseration. Sometimes there are no thaws, no defrost buttons. Sometimes we must simply wear the cold.

So many of us wore the cold that year. Each storm was a little different. Loved ones died. Jobs were lost. Marriages imploded. Cancers attacked. In the busy holiday season, we carried our pain to Sunday services and school concerts, cringing in the back rows while children's choirs sang of the "click, click, click" on the housetops and worship leaders compelled us to "go tell it on the mountain." We limped and grimaced and went through the motions, counting the disappearing links on the paper chains as a mercy.

A few days before Christmas, on the longest night of the year, my friends pulled into the driveway and trudged through the snow to my house. Inside, we had cleared the furniture, set up a Christmas tree, turned off the overhead lights, and lined the living room with a circle of chairs, a box of tissues under every seat. An Advent wreath in deep blues was in the middle of the room. We faced it and each other as our friend Jared pulled out his guitar and strummed the notes of "O Come, O Come, Emmanuel."

This was our makeshift Blue Christmas service. In our collective winters, we weren't immune to the holiness of the season. We wanted to hold together the mystery of the baby God born to us, but we needed a space where our prayers were set in a minor key and our worship could look like lament. We quietly read the opening prayer from a small leaflet on each chair.

Merciful God,
In this season of rejoicing, we come to you
weary and grieving.
In this season of feasting, we hunger for healing
and relief.
In this season of light, our hearts are veiled in
sorrow and shadow.
Will this season ever end?

"Yes." We hear your "Yes."
Those who are weary will find rest.
Those who mourn will be comforted.
Those who hunger will be filled.
The Light shines in the darkness,

and the darkness will not overcome it.[2]

We lit the candles, one by one, as Jared hummed the story of the ransomed captive Israel. The room glowed as we read Isaiah's and Jeremiah's promises of comfort to the broken-hearted, promises that the darkness would not last forever. We mourners in lonely exile pulled wooden ornaments off our tree, grabbed a marker, and hung our sorrows among twinkling lights. Some of the words on the ornaments were bold and beautiful: a testament to those loved and lost. *Elaine. Mom. William.* Other words were smudged, blurred with tears, or written in the tiny cursive of a secret shame. But there they were: prayers of lament on a Christmas tree, a communal honoring of solitary sorrows. In the dim light, we watched the tree and whispered "amen," believing the Son of God had appeared. Our laments were our offerings, and they were costly.

That night in my living room, our carols joined the songs of generations of mourning believers. Those who have gone before us lend language to our lament. From the bookshelf, John of the Cross and Ignatius of Loyola comfort us with names for our pain, names like "dark night of the soul" and "desolation." From the record player, we lament in song; ancient dirges and Negro spirituals gift us with the language of a bloodied but resilient faith.

> Sometimes I feel like a motherless child, a long way from home.
> Sometimes I feel like I'm almost done, a long way from home.
> True believer, a long way from home.[3]

In these timeworn laments, pain finds permission to take up space. We are here in the darkness; we are not the first, we are not the last, and our sorrow takes its place in the family of God. There is permission to bring the dark seasons of our lives to prayer. As George MacDonald writes,

> It is not the high summer alone that is God's. The winter is also His. And into His winter He came to visit us. And all man's winters are His—the winter of our poverty, the winter of our sorrow, the winter of our unhappiness—even "the winter of our discontent."[4]

Language for the winter of our sorrow also rises from the Word, which offers an entire book called Lamentations. Throughout the Bible, we see the heroes of the faith lean into the holy rhythms of lament. From Hannah in the temple to Jeremiah in the street, tears flow freely and agony takes time. In the foreword to *A Sacred Sorrow*, Eugene Peterson writes,

> Jesus wept. Job wept. David wept. Jeremiah wept. . . . But just try it yourself. Even, maybe especially, in church where these tear-soaked Scriptures are provided to shape our souls and form our behavior. Before you know it, a half-dozen men and women surround you with handkerchiefs, murmuring reassurances, telling you that it is going to be alright, intent on helping you "get over it." Why are Christians, of all people, embarrassed by tears, uneasy in the presence of sorrow, and unpracticed at the language of lament?[5]

It's a question that brings me uncomfortably close with myself.

In the winter, when it's too cold to have my quiet time outside, I turn my pantry into my prayer room. Imagine a hobbit hole. It's lined with shelves of bread and butter, and a small desk is built into the back-right corner. A miniature lamp provides just enough light to read. Drying herbs hang overhead like a garland. Under a shelf of essential oils, a small strip of corkboard holds Post-It note prayers and pictures of wildflowers. Each day during my long winter, I wrapped myself in a blanket, lit a patchouli candle, and turned on the light. "Here I am," I prayed. Then, I said nothing else.

At first, I tried to rally from my personal winter by opening Bible study books, buying new prayer journals, and printing prayer calendars. I was determined to claw my way out of my inner chill. But among the herbs, God came to me with a wintering kindness. It started with a story.[6] My memory of it is blurred (most of my memories from that season have a washed-out pall), but in my mind's eye it expanded, taking on new characters and dimensions. My own version goes something like this.

Once, there was a Jesuit priest who served as a spiritual director for a young monk. The young man came to their meetings with a broken heart, feeling depressed, lethargic, and far from God. "What do I do?" the man asked the old Jesuit. "How do I get out of this desolation? Guide me to some disciplines."

"Imagine there is a man in a sandstorm," the old priest replied, answering—as all good teachers do—with a parable. "He travels across the desert on a camel when a giant sandstorm overtakes him. The wind picks up, and a dark cloud engulfs him. He can't see. He can't breathe. He is sitting there on the back of a camel, exposed, being stung by sand. What should he do?"

The young man thought for a moment before responding. "He should get down from the camel, cover his head, and wait for the storm to pass." The older man nodded slowly. "Sometimes, the only way to survive a storm is to stop moving, wait for the darkness to pass, and—as best you can—try to enjoy being close to the ground."

In my pantry, Jesus invited me to get low. He didn't descend with a lesson, relieve my pain, or spur me to action. Instead, he pulled my blanket over my head and sat quietly with me. He was my Ground of Being; as best as I could,

I tried to enjoy being close. His patient presence was the consolation I needed.

Something in his quiet presence is reminiscent of Job's friends. Anyone familiar with the story knows that Job experienced unimaginable suffering. He lost his children, his livelihood, his health, his reputation, and his community. Blow after blow descended until we find him sitting in an ash pile, using a fragment of pottery to scrape at the sores on his diseased skin. When his friends heard what happened, they came to his house to show sympathy and comfort. The story says that when they saw him, he was so ravaged by grief, disease, and loss that he was almost unrecognizable.

Now, before long, Job's friends are going to be idiots. They'll make the fatal mistake of opening their mouths and trying to rationalize his pain. Surely there's a reason for such suffering, which means there must be a cure, which means Job needs to *do something* so this sorrow will go away. By the end of the book, God has some very poignant words for their presumptions.

But before they start moralizing, they do something beautiful. The Word tells us that when they saw his shattered body oozing in the ashes, "they raised their voices and wept, and they tore their robes and sprinkled dust on their heads toward heaven" (Job 2:12 ESV). They didn't clean him up. They didn't silence his cries. They got down in the ashes with their friend and let their tears mingle with his.

The story continues, "They sat with him on the ground seven days and seven nights, and no one spoke a word to him, for they saw his suffering was very great" (v. 13 ESV). Seven days and seven nights. What a radical act of kindness and solidarity. These men had lives: families, job responsibilities, demanding daily rhythms. And though the story doesn't specify their ages (except to say that one friend was younger), it is implied that these are not young men. I'm in my forties, and if I sleep with the wrong pillow, my neck hurts for a month. These old men got down on the ground. They sacrificed their time, energy, and physical comfort to meet Job in his suffering. It cost them something. For a whole week, they were silent comrades to his pain. They never said a word until he did.

Yet the pull of an explanation is hard to resist. Eventually, Job's friends begin hypothesizing about his suffering, desperate to contextualize the evils that befell Job. I get it. When I hear about a freak accident or a scary diagnosis, I scramble for details, as if understanding what caused someone else's suffering will help me distance it from my own reality. Being a patient participant in lament is an acknowledgment of our own vulnerability.

Once, in the prayer room of a nearby church, our small group practiced lament. We wrote our own psalms like Psalm 88, without a happy ending. In the corner of the room was a small altar, carefully crafted from an old pine cabinet, a lace doily, and frankincense oil. We read our handwritten laments out loud, then knelt at the altar and laid them at the foot of the cross.

The witnesses in the room were instructed to be still, just like Job's friends. When a lament was read, we weren't allowed to pass Kleenex, offer reassurances, or even pat the person on the shoulder.

Those soothing gestures, though kindly intended, were like the attempts of the fabled Dutch boy who put his fingers in a leaking dike. Our job was not to stop up the flow of sorrow. Our act of solidarity was to bear witness to grief and let it take all the space it needed.

I remember the day my youngest son bit his lower lip, turned on his heels, and fled the middle school building. I followed him out, watching him shake his head and look up at the clouds in an attempt to keep from crying. It had been a long day at a school competition. Emotions ran high, disappointments hung heavy, and sharp words had passed between friends. He squatted under the eave of the building, avoiding the puddles of rain, as I knelt beside him.

He wasn't ready to talk. He didn't want to be touched. Later, when we got home, he closed the door to his room and pulled his blanket over his head. When he was ready, I joined him, crawling into the bottom bunk and wrapping my arm around the wad of blankets and stuffies that surrounded my son.

"Did you know that tears tell stories?" I asked him. "Some tears are worker tears that keep our eyes from getting too dry. Some tears are cleaner tears that get rid of dust or sand. Those tears are mostly made up of water. But there are also feeler tears. Those tears aren't just water. They're full of toxins and stress hormones and all our body's responses to our sad stories. When we cry, we let them out. So if you want to cry," I whispered into the pile of stuffed animals, "it would be okay."

It was a good speech, but if I'm being honest, I was preaching to myself. For all my counseling courses and hours in contemplative prayer, my own tears still leave me a bit like Eugene Peterson's churchgoer, passing myself a hankie and a cue to "get over it." Learning to make peace with my sorrows has been a hard-won mercy.

When I struggle to find value in my laments, I cling to the image of God in Psalm 56. In that psalm, David prays: "You have seen me tossing and turning through the night. You have collected all my tears and preserved them in your bottle! You have recorded every one in your book" (v. 8 TLB). What tender validation of our suffering. I imagine God surrounded by shelves of sparkling bottles—green and blue, clear and silver. Each bottle contains a collection of tears composed of stress hormones and stories. God patiently writes each sorrow in his book, honoring and treasuring each costly act of lament as worship. In his presence, I find the perfect container for my pain.

In 1 Thessalonians 4, Paul points mourners to Jesus, to his second advent when he will return with a "soul-stirring cry" (v. 16 TLB) and snatch us to his side. I wonder—will we enter his room of bottles? Will his tears mingle with ours? Will we watch him write our pain in his book? Lament is a chapter worth reading slowly, but thank God, our pain never has the final word. And so we sing. O come, O come, Emmanuel.

PRACTICE: LAMENT TOOLS

Every sorrow is unique, and every stage of grief requires different care. Below is a list of lament tools referenced in the chapter.

1. **Sit in the sandstorm.** This practice offers the gift of space. All you need is a blanket and a quiet room. Wrap the blanket around your shoulders or over your head. Take a deep breath and become aware of God's presence with you. Pray, "Lord, here I am." Sit with him in silence until you feel satisfied, then close your time with "amen."
2. **Write a psalm of lament.** You will need a Bible, notebook, and pen for this practice. Read Psalm 13. Consider the sorrows and struggles you carry. Dump your thoughts on the page without censoring or organizing. Then take those words and form them into a short poem. When you are finished, pray your psalm to the Lord. This practice can be done in one sitting or over days or weeks.
3. **Find a friend.** Lamenting in community offers consolation, support, and witness. Consider writing a

psalm of lament and sharing it with a spiritual director or trusted friend. Be sure to share with someone who will listen well, honor your suffering (not try to resolve it), and allow space for your first-draft emotions.

4. **Make a playlist.** Music lends language to lament when we can't find words. Make a playlist of sorrow songs. This playlist serves as a script for prayer. Turn your awareness to God, listen to the music, and let the songs pray for you.

12

THE CORNER OF THIRD AND VINE

Discernment in Prayer

> Getting answers to my questions is not the goal of the spiritual life. Living in the presence of God is the greater call.
>
> Henri Nouwen[1]

On the bottom ledge of my bookshelf, under *The Bell Jar* and *A Man Called Ove*, is an unvarnished wooden box. It's my "fire item," the one thing I would save if the house were burning. On the lid, a hand-carved garland of laurel leaves encircles my name. The bronze latch on the left side never fully locks, and if you tilt your head at just the right angle, you can catch a glimpse of the treasures inside.

Admittedly, the contents are precious only to me. If my sons heard me allude to treasures, they would be disappointed. No gold doubloons or World War II medals hide inside—only multicolored papers and tatty old ribbons. But to me, it is a collection of the dearest things: Crayola rainbows and handprint flowers, love notes on gas station receipts, and happy prayers on a Muir Woods brochure. I hoard the words and bind them in twine.

An essay prompt recently sparked a memory, and I reached for the box. Shuffling past the birthday cards and magazine clippings, I found what I was looking for: a crisp white envelope with "Clearness Committee" in the upper right corner. As I emptied its contents on the desk, I was struck by the handwriting. Each page was different, and each page was familiar. The irregular bends of my mother's capital *H*. The loopy ampersand that joins Ashley's words. The green doodles in the corner of my sister's notes. There, in every shade of ink, were my people. Without reading a single word, I was back in the chapel on a warm spring evening five years ago.

I'm not sure who lit the incense, but it was probably Evan. Generously, he offered the use of the Old Baptist Church on the corner of Third and Vine. As we ambled into the dark building with its stained-glass windows and creaky wood floors, the smell of frankincense followed us to a circle of chairs.

After we found our seats, Hannah smiled warmly and began. "Welcome to Laura's Clearness Committee. We're here tonight because we love Laura and the whole Kauffman family. Since Micah starts kindergarten this fall, Laura seeks discernment on what to do with her time during the school day. She senses that God is inviting her to write. She wants her community—you guys—to help her discern God's invitation."

The rules of a clearness committee are simple: Pull up a chair. Listen to the focus person describe the discernment they seek. Listen for the traces of the Holy Spirit. Hold silence. Then, slowly, ask open-ended questions or reflect the focus person's statements verbatim. Advice is forbidden, and suggestions are frowned upon. The work of the committee is to listen.

In an introductory monologue, the focus person begins by naming their need for discernment in one short sentence. "I want to discern if God is calling me to the vocation of writing," I told my friends. After the discernment sentence, the focus person fills in the picture. As I reflected on my life, I traced a thread of longing. Words had always been precious to me; since childhood, writing had connected me to God. My mom grinned as I recounted stories of the love poems I wrote to Jesus in the fourth grade and the Bible study curriculum I developed at the wise old age of twelve. Writing was my language, but I had stopped speaking it. Life had happened. I became a counselor, had children, and taught prayer groups. I managed doctor's appointments, filled the fridge, and refereed Nerf wars. For a hot minute, I even sold antiques because why not? In a vocation with so many twists and turns, was "writing" a calling or a diversion? Nothing in my life qualified me to claim the title "writer." Except, of course, desire.

Asking my friends to spend an evening focused on me felt strange and maybe even presumptuous. Sending out the invitations for my clearness committee was a battle against my darker angels. With a few keystrokes, I fought the lies of insecurity (*This is a big ask.*), shame (*So much self-absorption, Laura. Get over yourself.*), and embarrassment (*Aren't you making a big deal about nothing?*).

William Barry illustrates this inner tension when he writes,

> When a person asks himself what most frequently prevents him from doing good, he may find that it is not impulses to evil, but a fear that he will be thought of as different by his friends and colleagues. . . . Inner arguments that persistently succeed in preventing us from responding to God are exceptionally hardy . . . [they] seldom lead to answers and consistently stop movement toward God.[2]

My inner arguments might have held sway were it not for Hannah. Years before she welcomed my group of friends to the Old Baptist Church, she invited me to her own clearness committee. Sitting cross-legged on the floor, I listened as she told her story and named her need for discernment. It wasn't indulgent; it was intentional. Opening her life to her community was an act of bravery and humility. I was honored to pray with her. All the lies that tried to dissuade me from assembling my own clearness committee fell flat in light of my faithful friend.

The Quaker practice of the clearness committee appealed to me for its communality. All the major decisions of my life had happened somewhat informally. College. Grad school. Moves. Even when I got married and had kids, the process was organic. There were personal prayers and a smattering of conversations with family, but the decisions happened over time, with each day of dating or each year of marriage bringing us closer to a choice. There is a quiet beauty to this slow, accidental discernment, but I found a formality in the clearness committee that appealed to me. The shared prayer time gave structure and intention to my decision-making. The people I trust the most in the world sat in a circle for two hours, listened to my story, asked questions, and affirmed the Spirit in me.

What they didn't do was expect me to reach a decision. The clearness committee isn't overly concerned with a conclusion. After all, as the saying goes, "If we are seeking God for our own good and profit, we are not seeking God."[3] We don't approach God as a Magic 8-Ball, something to listen to our questions and make an answer appear in the window of our blue-inked confusion. The goal of discernment isn't "right choice" as much as "right relationship." Clarity in the clearness committee is less about a decision and more about an awareness of God's presence in the decision-making process.

There's a mercy here. If the chief goal of discernment is to make the right decision (about a job change, a cross-country move, or a relationship), the practice would be fraught. *What if I get it wrong?* It would be easy for discernment to feel like a spiritual test. Hear God correctly and get a gold star. Did things not work out so great on the decision you made? Epic spiritual fail. Instead, discernment invites us to hold our answers with holy detachment so that we might faithfully "live the questions."[4]

Of course, there are times we don't need discernment. If my kid comes to me weighing whether or not to hit his brother for stealing his toy, the answer is always no. The Spirit makes God's will known through the Word, the family of God, and the created world. Living congruently with the ways of God is always the right decision. The kind of discernment found in contemplative prayer goes beyond the choice between "good and bad" and into the world of the "good and also good." Discernment, in this context, is a practice of freedom.

At my private Christian college, there was a sidewalk between the freshman boys' dorm and the freshman girls' dorm that we commonly referred to as "The Meet Market" (or, for the more jaded among us, "The Meat Market"). The boys, who always had guitars, chatted up the girls, who always wore cross necklaces. With the chords of the latest worship songs purring in the background, the freshmen masses tried their luck with a handful of Christianese pickup lines. The inanity of these holy come-ons cannot be overstated, but the absolute worst line was as simple as it was ridiculous: "Heeeey, so, I'm pretty sure God told me we should date."

Now, I'm telling this story tongue in cheek. I'm a woman in my forties, but I remember what it was like to be an overly sincere, hormone-plagued college kid. No judgment on those poor teens saying stupid stuff. I get it—it's tough out there. But I still remember when one earnest friend told me he had prayed a lot and was sure God wanted us to be together. I thought, *Well . . . it seems like one of us is hearing God wrong. I'm going to assume it's you.*

We've all seen a version of this, right? In the name of hearing from God, people make strange demands on others' money, time, or energy. Think of shiny-faced televangelists asking for donations or collection plates passed at the height of worship. Too often, well-meaning (and sometimes not so well-meaning) leaders justify self-serving or even harmful behavior in the name of the Lord, saying they're responding to his voice. Like my college-aged self, we listen to their pleas and think, *It seems like one of us is hearing God wrong. I'm going to assume it's you.* Because of its often-unintended abuses, discernment can get a bad rap.

The kind of discernment we pursue in contemplative prayer has a different intent and energy than that of a college romantic or televangelist. *Discernment* is the quality of being able to perceive the hidden. When placed in the context of contemplative prayer, it is anchored in freedom, attention, and patience. Traits like certainty, restrictiveness, and prescription take a back seat. Instead of looking for answers, discernment begins with a question and ends with a conversation. Nothing is too small to escape our sparrow-seeing God's concern, and nothing is so large it might overwhelm the Rock of Ages. Everything that stirs in our spirits or on our horizon is a catalyst for prayer.

Back in the Old Baptist Church, I concluded my introductory monologue for my clearness committee. It was time for the group members to respond. As I passed the metaphorical microphone to my friends, I anxiously awaited questions about my doubts and qualifications. But the fears, which felt all-consuming in my personal narrative, were not what had resonated with the members of my clearness committee—not even close. One by one, my people read their notes aloud.

"Laura, you said that Jesus was the birthplace of your words," Megan began. As is customary in contemplative practices, we paused and let those words take up space.

After a while, my mother offered, "You told us that when you write, you see the face of God." We paused again. We breathed.

"Laura said, 'I want to meet God in the wild, raw, unpredictable places. I want to write about it. Also, I would like to stay sane,'" Ashley commented. (She drew a cheeky little smiley face next to that last bit in her notes.)

As the clearness committee drew to a close on that soft spring night, we were quiet. We had spoken enough; it was time to listen. "What is my calling?" I asked Jesus in the candlelight. "What would you have me do?"

As he so often does, God spoke to my imagination. The dusky church morphed into the throne room, where I sat at Jesus's feet. I couldn't stop looking at him. He was beautiful—so heartbreakingly, earthshakingly beautiful. You could spend every minute of a lifetime and every word of a dictionary trying to describe him without even scratching the surface. *But*, I thought, as I sat at his feet, *wouldn't it be fun to try?*

Yes, yes. He laughed in response. *You are my little scribe.*

I entered the clearness committee looking for practical answers: how to spend my time, what kind of work to do, and how to steward my career. Instead of speaking to my output or action, God answered the questions I hadn't known to ask. *Let's push Pause on what to* do, he said. *Let's start with who we* are. Richard Rohr is right: When I got my "Who am I?" question right, all of my "What should I do?" questions took care of themselves.[5]

When we are rooted in our identity and richly connected to who God is, action becomes an expression of holy freedom. All is a response to a centered friendship with God. Win or lose, succeed or fail, we walk the road together. It is enough.

PRACTICE: DISCERNMENT AND THE MERTON PRAYER

Tools for discernment can be as communal as the clearness committee and as solitary as personal prayer. The practice below works well in a small group or on your own. Whether you are seeking general wisdom (*How then should I live?*) or specific discernment (*Should I accept this job offer?*), this tool enables prayerful engagement with the decision-making process.

Leaning on a prayer from Thomas Merton, we pray over our concern in three "movements."[6] Think of them like the movements of a Beethoven sonata or stanzas in a poem. We read, pause, and respond, then proceed to the next movement.

1. **Settle** into prayer. Let your mind and body be still. Breathe deeply. Become aware that you are in the presence of the Father, Son, and Holy Spirit.
   Inhale: "Your sheep know your voice." Exhale: "I rest in your guidance."
2. **Slowly read** a movement of Merton's prayer aloud. Pause after any phrase that grabs your attention. Then, consider the reflection question. Jot a response if you'd like, but resist the urge to journal; keep your

answers short. When you feel satisfied, move to the next movement.

Movement One

My Lord God,
I have no idea where I am going.
I do not see the road ahead of me.
I cannot know for certain where it will end
nor do I really know myself,
and the fact that I think I am following your will
does not mean that I am actually doing so.

Consider the road ahead of you. Name it in prayer.

Movement Two

But I believe that the desire to please you
does in fact please you.
And I hope I have that desire
in all that I am doing.
I hope that I will never do anything
apart from that desire.

Your desire to please God pleases God. How does that reality affect your heart, mind, or body?

Movement Three

And I know that if I do this you will lead me by
the right road,
though I may know nothing about it.
Therefore will I trust you always though
I may seem to be lost and in the shadow of death.
I will not fear, for you are ever with me,
and you will never leave me to face my perils alone.

What's it like to pray this last movement?

3. **Close the prayer.** Take a few deep breaths. Tell God what this exercise was like for you. Repeat the breath prayer from the beginning.

   Inhale: "Your sheep know your voice." Exhale: "I rest in your guidance."

   Allow for extended silence.

13

THE FALLOW SEASON

Closing Prayer

Out on the edge, you can see all kinds of things you can't see from the center.

Kurt Vonnegut[1]

Every year, near the end of autumn, the cottonwoods turn gold, the winged spindles turn red, and the mornings turn cold. The geese form vees overhead, so high their migration calls are quiet, like an echo across a canyon. The combine harvesters march in rows to the cornfields, and their dust hangs heavy in the cooling air. Everything, from the ground to the sky, shows the signs of the changing season, but it still surprises me to wake up and find the first frost on the lawn.

If the forecast is to be believed, the temperate days are numbered. Last weekend, I decided it was time to prepare the garden bed for winter. Armed with my rake and work gloves, I pulled tomato plants from the ground, one after another, until the wheelbarrow overflowed with rotting fruit. The lemon balm required a shovel to pry it loose, but the cornstalks came free with the slightest tug. For hours, I wrenched my garden from the earth. There was a sharp scent of garlic and tomato in the air, and my back ached from hunching over the remaining weeds between the rows.

Dusk in the garden came faster than usual—yet another predictable surprise. I pulled on a sweater in the fading light and surveyed my work from the edge of the garden. Everything was bare. Just that morning the beds had been overgrown with summer excess; now they were empty and clean. Straight lines from the metal rake covered the ground. After months of adding compost to the soil, choosing and planting seeds, watering the beds, endlessly weeding, and chasing the dogs away from the mulch, there was nothing left to do but say thank you and wait for the winter.

I'm not well suited for winter. The energy of springtime planting appeals to me, as does the bustle of summer maintenance and harvest. At the risk of being an American cliché, I find myself more at home in planning and production than in completion and rest. I tend to ask "What's next?" instead of "What's here?" The autumn invites me to prepare for the fallow season of winter. It forces me to unscrew the hose, lay my plants on the compost heap, and trust that the work was enough. In its changing rhythm, autumn becomes my spiritual discipline.

Every year, starting in October, I reread Katherine May's *Wintering*. It's my rake and shovel, preparing me to embrace the season of contentment. "Plants and animals don't fight the winter," she reminds me;

> they don't pretend it's not happening and attempt to carry on living the same lives that they lived in the summer. They prepare. They adapt. They perform extraordinary acts of metamorphosis to get them through. Winter is a time of withdrawing from the world, maximizing scant resources, carrying out acts of brutal efficiency and vanishing from sight; but that's where the transformation occurs. Winter is not the death of the life cycle, but its crucible.[2]

After emptying the wheelbarrow, I propped my muck boots by the door and washed garden dirt from under my nails for the last time of the season. There's a sorrow to completion. As dirt flowed down the drain, I took stock of the garden I'd just closed. The lavender had spread like wildfire, the pumpkins had been ruined by squash vine borer, and the cherry tomatoes had been so prolific I couldn't keep up. Wasps had gutted the overripe watermelons when I didn't harvest them quickly enough, and the clematis had bloomed with the prettiest flowers I'd ever seen. At the sink, I closed my garden again—not with my rake but with my attention.

Moments of closure like these feel rare. Life seems to heave with momentum, propelling me from one moment to the next. Events and activities blur together. Even though the world is full of nighttime and winters, I don't easily heed the natural endings. Like a computer that idles but is never shut down, my life is a browser of open tabs. Paused, perhaps, but not often closed. Drying my hands on a towel, I notice that closure is akin to surrender. There's a mercy in a boundary line.

Too often, I live in the world of "one more thing." In the garden, I imagine what might have been, tallying up chores that never got completed and strawberries I never got to eat. At bedtime, I rehearse a list of "shoulds": the phone calls I should have made, the workout I should have done, the moments of connection I should have savored with my boys. I leave the tabs open because I do not trust that the work I've done is enough.

Even in prayer, I am not immune to the pull of *more.* There are always more people I could have prayed for, more discernment I could have sought, more practices I could have tried. Choosing to close the tab on my garden, my day, and even my time in prayer is a discipline, a line in the sand saying the work is done, and it was enough for now.

It was the cherry tomato that got me there this time. The flow of shoulds stopped abruptly when—without thinking—I popped the last cherry tomato into my mouth. There is nothing like the meaty taste of a tomato pulled straight from the plant.

"Oh man, that's so good," I groaned, and my spirit shifted. Had my garden been perfect? No. The grapes didn't produce, the carpetweed overtook the poppies, and I've already told you about the pumpkins. But it didn't matter. I spent hours in the clean air, cultivating freckles and laughing at the crazy spirals that grew from the random plant Micah picked out from the local nursery. There were roses and zinnias and sweet red peppers. I could close my season with a list of shoulds, or I could wipe tomato juice from my lips and say thank you.

There are moments when we detect the signs of the changing season, and prayer includes such moments. Of course, we pray without ceasing; the sun shines on the soil no matter the season. But each hour of spiritual direction ends, each spoken prayer grows quiet, and each sequestered moment with God ushers us out to serve the world.

Like a first frost or skein of geese, we recognize the signs that the active work of prayer is slanting toward closure. Sometimes it's internal: a settling of the soil and a sense of completion. Other times it's practical: the baby wakes up, the clock strikes seven, or the phone rings. Either way, we know it is time to transition.

At this point, we have a choice. We can leave the tab open, mentally rehearsing all that still needs to be done in prayer, or we can say thank you and believe it was enough for now. In ending well, closure becomes an act of trust.

How do your prayers usually end? Do you journal? Open your eyes? Say the Lord's Prayer?

Admittedly, I'm a drifter. I don't often pray out loud, so my prayers happen in my inner world, where my thoughts drift from a conversation with God (*I had a sweet moment with Lucas on the car ride to school today. Thank you for that.*) to memory (*The road was so bumpy; when are they going to grade the gravel?*) to to-dos (*With roads like that, I need to get the tires checked soon.*). Then I reach for my phone to look up the number of the closest mechanic, and my prayer has unceremoniously come to a close.

It took me years (and a little therapy) to accept this as normal. My mind works like all other human minds do, and God will meet me in my search engine as well as in my oratory. Instead of shaming me for my wandering mind, God invites me to a little laughter. Of course, there is always room to grow, but if I can't laugh about a prayer ending in tire rotation, I'm missing out. Turns out a sense of humor can be a spiritual discipline too.

In contemplative prayer, closure can be as simple as an "amen" and as complex as a full review of our time with God. Whatever form we choose, our closure always begins with a pause, which probably comes as no surprise. By now, the pause of attention has become our home base. In ending, it's our moment at the sink, with dirt under our nails, to look back at what happened in our time with God.

Blame it on my love of symmetry, but the contemplative tool I use the most for closing prayer is another iteration of The Two Questions. Remember chapter 5, and the two questions Sherri taught me to ask at the beginning of prayer? The Spiritual Exercises extend two more questions for the end of prayer, a sort of bookend to our intentional time spent with God.

"As you close, you might like to say the Lord's Prayer," Sherri said when she introduced me to the Exercises' daily rhythm. "Then, pull out your journal and consider these two questions. Question one: 'How did I experience God?' Remember, there is no wrong answer. Simply reflect and respond in one short sentence. Then move to question two: 'How did God experience me?'"

During my journey through the Spiritual Exercises, I answered those questions every day for nine months. At the end of prayer, I'd pause, reflect on what happened, and jot my answers in my journal. Then, in the way you do, I'd forget about them. Life filled up with activity and the mental load of dog-feeding, session-keeping, clothes-cleaning, and child-rearing. After a quick sitcom to lull me to sleep and an early alarm for prayer, I'd open my journal with a sleepy, unfocused gaze. The experiences of yesterday might as well have been a lifetime ago.

But the words remained. One day, as the nine months slanted toward closure, I grabbed my journal and prepared to end my journey through the Spiritual Exercises. Mercifully, it was the afternoon and I was sufficiently caffeinated. There at my fingertips was a record of everything God had been to me in prayer for the better part of a year. I laughed at some of my responses, remembering times God came to me as a playmate or a bumblebee at the window. I sighed over others, remembering when God was my Comforter, Man of Sorrows, and Tear-Collector. Grabbing a blank sheet of paper, I transcribed every response into a master list, compiling my experiences of God in one massive inventory. By the third page, I was weeping. Did I have shoulds for my spiritual life? Sure. But how could I hold them with the taste of such sweet fruit in my mouth?

The question about how God experienced me was harder to answer. I didn't want to arbitrarily write a biblical truth about God's general heart toward humankind (though there is a time and a place for that). I wanted something beyond recitation; I wanted reaction.

Of course, God's heart never changes; he always sees us as beloved children, in the same way my heart toward my kids is always that of a loving mom. But while my heart is constant, my experience changes from moment to moment. Fresh emotions stir when I see my boys perform at a recital, drop a football pass, or help each other when one of them falls. My character is constant, but my experience is dynamic. So with God. He is unchanging but not static; he is responsive and nuanced.

In my journal, after the opening words "God experienced me as . . . ," there were a lot of entries that simply ended with a question mark. I didn't know how God was experiencing me. The work of asking and listening takes time, and I'm still learning to hear. The yields of this question have been slow-growing, but my list is getting longer. There may have been days that resulted in question marks, but there were also a few hard-won answers, days when God experienced me as his "beloved," "little sister," and "coworker." They are truths that grow on the vine of the Word, but they taste so much sweeter when taken from the hand of God.

The Two Questions close a time of prayer with the assumption of divine connection. Because no matter how focused or distracted we feel, no matter how connected or distant God seems, no matter how productive or quiet our time in prayer is, God is there, experiencing us. And whether we are aware of it or not, we are experiencing God too. Every act of attention stakes us in God's fertile garden; every act of prayer wraps cords of connection around our hearts and his, binding us together in a love that will never end. The work is done, and indeed it is enough.

On the back patio, we have a birdfeeder filled with a "wild Midwest blend feed." It's mostly a hodgepodge of millet and corn, but the birds' favorite part seems to be the black oil sunflower seeds. We watch them dig through the tray, sending kernels flying, until they reach the prized seeds at the bottom.

A sunflower sprouted in my landscaping after a cardinal battle at the feeder and a few good rains. So did a carnival squash, which I had never heard of. Despite all my cultivating, the birds had minds of their own. We didn't get to eat the watermelon I tended, but we did put that sunflower in a vase on the table. The harvest is out of our hands.

In prayer, we cultivate the soil of our souls. We plant and water, asking for discernment, lingering in the Word, and practicing the discipline of silence. But there's no saying what will grow. The Spirit wheels wildly through our prayers, always full of life but not often predictable. There's such kindness here: Prayer is not our garden, and we don't control the sun. What will be will be.

Paul said it this way: "I planted the seed, Apollos watered it, but God has been making it grow" (1 Cor. 3:6). In prayer, we kneel beside God in the warm soil of his love. We watch him work; we learn from him. With those "unforced rhythms of grace" (Matt. 11:29 MSG), we follow his lead, seeing how he does it. The work of prayer is its own reward, and mercifully, the outcomes are not our responsibility. Every good fruit is an act of Jesus's generosity to us. As Thomas Merton says, contemplation is "a theological grace. It can come to us only as a gift, and not as a result of our own clever use of spiritual techniques."[3]

Look for the cherry tomato and set down the shoulds. Wash your hands and say thank you.

God is with you. Rest in these promises, and be at peace.

Like the world outside my window, this book is in its autumn. Writing has felt so similar to gardening: planting ideas, wondering if anything will actually grow, pulling out the conceptual weeds, and watching the words sprout on the page. "You can plant. Your editor can water. But I'll make it grow," God promised. Now, in the autumn of this work, I feel the soil settle. There's a sorrow to completion, indeed.

We've tended these pages together, you and I, as writer and reader. At the beginning of the book, we dug into our spiritual heritage, lingered in God's loving gaze, and cultivated Sabbath. As prayer grew, we nurtured the soil of ourselves, identified desires, and feasted on the Word of God.

We sought burning bushes, joined God at play, and encountered Christ in our flesh and bone. In the dusk of prayer, we stood on the shoulders of the saints, prayed in the dark, and discerned the movements of God.

Now, on the edge of the book, we look back and take stock. I'm dirty and tired; the work has been demanding and rich. The harvest feels surprising—so different from what I planted. "Is it enough?" I ask God. "Should I have done it differently?"

Who cares, he says, popping a cherry tomato in his mouth. *It was all prayer, and that's enough for now.*

I'm learning to love the ground that lies
beneath my feet in the fallow season:

the ground of the dormant, of sleeping life
that carries no promise of certain production

the ground of the nourished, fed by the death
of the things that once bloomed

the ground of the passive, that simply receives
the rains of the fall and the rest of winter

the ground that cannot be measured
by the brightness of green breaking the rows

or the richness of fruits that fall from the vines
or the service it pays to some greater end

but holds its value in the simple act
of embracing its wild and wonderful *being*.[4]

PRACTICE: CENTERING PRAYER

Centering prayer was developed by Thomas Keating in the 1970s, but its roots trace back to the early Christian church. Since the days of the desert mothers and fathers, believers have cultivated interior silence as a way of being still and knowing God (Ps. 46).

In centering prayer, we release "more" and embrace "less." We trust that as we quiet our hearts and minds, we find Jesus in the silence. He meets us there and receives our stillness as worship.

To begin, set a timer (I recommend five minutes), and move through the following steps:

1. **Choose** a word for your prayer time: a name for God, a phrase from the Bible, or a short prayer (3–4 words max).
2. **Sink** into prayer. Take a deep breath. Let your mind grow still. Imagine you are a scuba diver, sinking deeper and deeper into God's love.
3. **Return** to your word or phrase when thoughts pop up (which they will). Repeat it and let it serve as an anchor, pulling you deeper into an awareness of God.

4. **Rise** back. When your timer chimes or your spirit is satisfied, let your attention float back to the world. Slowly open your eyes. End your time in silence, surrounded by the love of God.

BENEDICTION

My Blessing for the Reader

May you unearth deep roots:
may your love for Jesus be richly blessed
by your heritage in the family of God.

May you be present to the Presence:
may you sense that the loving gaze of God
follows you all the days of your life.

May your prayers become a Sabbath:
may you breathe free in God's easy yoke
and find rest for your weary soul.

May you know the ground of yourself:
may you hear the God of the garden
singing over you with joy.

May you receive the desires of your heart:
may your longings find a home with Christ
as you follow him freely down the road.

May you savor the flavors of God's table:
may the Scripture nourish and delight you
as you hunger and thirst for him.

May you find bushes burning everywhere:
    may holy attention leave you astonished
    and may love bloom brightly in response.

May your prayers be playful, creative, and free:
    may nothing prevent you from coming
    to Jesus's welcoming side.

May you trace God's contours in flesh and bone:
    may you sense his delight in your physical form
    and meet him in the temple of your skin.

May you stand on the shoulders of the saints:
    may the journey of those who've walked before you
    strengthen you on your way.

May you find grace to pray in the dark:
    may your tears fall on the feet of Christ
    as he bottles every one.

May you know the voice of the Shepherd:
    may holy freedom be your home
    and God's gentle words, your guide.

May you close your prayers in the harvest of peace:
    for every moment is holy
    and all of life is prayer.

ACKNOWLEDGMENTS

Writing may be a solitary task—a quiet room, butt in the chair, hands on the keys—but no one writes alone. This book has been bolstered by the insight, brilliance, and faith of countless individuals, from Ignatius of Loyola to my mom.

Thank you to the publishing team at Baker Books for your expertise and insight. Special thanks to my editor, Rachel Welcher, who sparked the idea for the book and faithfully championed my voice. What a privilege to cross the finish line together.

Thanks to Sustainable Faith for creating a space where professional excellence is rooted in love for God and others. I am especially grateful for the Des Moines cohort of the School of Spiritual Direction and its unmatchable instructors, Renae Norwood, Mike Harder, and Sherri Harder.

Sherri, for once, I'm at a loss for words. Thank you for showing me where to find the Bread.

A huge thanks to the friends and fellow writers who read early drafts, especially Hannah Estabrook, Ashley Smiley, John Blase, Nancy Bartelt, and Jen Riddle. You kept me going. You kept me grounded. You knew this was enough for now.

To Chris and the boys—thanks for rallying around me so I could do this. Thanks for being patient, for doing the dishes, for marching around the living room chanting "Dr. Mommy" when I got into the writing program. You four are the stuff of dreams.

My God, what a list; every day with you is Christmas. Thank you for receiving my simple words as love.

NOTES

Author's Note

1. Mary Oliver, "The Summer Day," *Devotions: The Selected Poems of Mary Oliver* (Penguin, 2017), 316.

2. The Porter's Gate, feat. Andrew Peterson and Leslie Jordan, "Centering Prayer," *Sanctuary Songs* (© 2023 The Porter's Gate), digital.

Chapter 1 Deep Roots

1. Flannery O'Connor, *Mystery and Manners: Occasional Prose* (Farrar, Straus & Giroux, 1970), 48.

2. David G. Benner, *Sacred Companions: The Gift of Spiritual Friendship & Direction* (InterVarsity, 2004), 17.

Chapter 2 Present to the Presence

1. Brother Lawrence, *The Practice of the Presence of God* (Whitaker House, 1982), 61.

2. Richard Rohr, *What the Mystics Know: Seven Pathways to Your Deeper Self* (Crossroad, 2019), 10.

3. J. R. R. Tolkien, *The Fellowship of the Ring* (Del Rey, 1986), 34.

4. Max Lucado, *Just Like Jesus: A Heart Like His* (Thomas Nelson, 2012), 64.

5. Walter Brueggemann, *Sabbath as Resistance: Saying No to the Culture of Now*, new ed. (Westminster John Knox, 2017), 45.

Chapter 3 Be Still

1. Susannah Heschel, "Introduction," in Abraham Joshua Heschel, *The Sabbath* (Farrar, Straus & Giroux, 2005), xiv.

2. Ruth Haley Barton, *Sacred Rhythms: Arranging Our Lives for Spiritual Transformation* (InterVarsity, 2006), 37.

3. See Patrick D. Miller, *The Ten Commandments: Interpretation: Resources for the Use of Scripture in the Church* (Westminster John Knox, 2009), 117.

Chapter 4 At Home

1. Wendell Berry, "How to Be a Poet," *Given: Poems* (Counterpoint, 2006), 18.

2. The kidneys were considered the seat of emotion in the ancient Near East, comparable to our use of "heart" in referring to the emotional self.

3. Sally Lloyd-Jones, *The Jesus Storybook Bible: Every Story Whispers His Name* (Zonderkidz, 2007), 220.

4. Authored by Dave Nixon of Sustainable Faith, https://sustainablefaith.com. Used by permission.

Chapter 5 The Flower Farm

1. Rainer Maria Rilke, "I, 59: Go to the Limits of Your Longing," in *Rilke's Book of Hours: Love Poems to God*, trans. Anita Barrows and Joanna Macy (Riverhead Books, 1996), 88.

2. Ignatius of Loyola, *Spiritual Exercises*.

3. Augustine, *Tractates on the First Letter of John*, 4.4.

4. David G. Benner, *Opening to God: Lectio Divina and Life as Prayer* (InterVarsity, 2021), 44–45.

5. John Calvin, *Institutes of the Christian Religion*, ed. John T. McNeill, trans. Ford Lewis Battles, vol. 1, The Library of Christian Classics (Westminster John Knox, 2011), 35.

Chapter 6 Sobre Mesa

1. Virginia Woolf, *A Room of One's Own: With an Introductory Essay "Professions for Women"* (Read Books Limited, 2017), 18.

2. For more information about La Salsamenta, visit https://lasalsamenta.com/.

3. For a beautiful and thorough discussion of stages of faith, I recommend Janet O. Hagberg and Robert A. Guelich, *The Critical Journey: Stages in the Life of Faith* (Sheffield Publishing, 2005).

4. Guigo II, *The Ladder of Monks: A Letter on the Contemplative Life and Twelve Meditations*, trans. Edmund Colledge and James Walsh, vol. 48, Cistercian Studies series (Liturgical Press, 1979), 69.

Chapter 7 Burning Bushes Everywhere

1. Blaise Pascal, *Pensées*, trans. A. J. Krailsheimer (Penguin, 1995), 142.

2. Mary Oliver, "Sometimes," *Red Bird: Poems* (Beacon Press, 2008), 35–38.

3. Mary Oliver, "Yes! No!," *White Pine: Poems and Prose Poems* (Harcourt Brace, 1994), 8.

4. Elizabeth Barrett Browning, *Aurora Leigh: A Poem in Nine Books* (T. Y. Crowell, 1883), 304.

5. Jon Guerra, "What Is Your Name?," *Keeper of Days* (© 2020 Thorndale Records), digital.

6. John Mark McMillan, "The Road, the Rocks, and the Weeds," *Peopled with Dreams* (© 2019 lionhawk Records), digital.

Chapter 8 Pure Imagination

1. Dora M. Kalff, "Introduction to Sandplay Therapy," *Journal of Sandplay Therapy* 1, no. 1 (Autumn 1991): 12, www.csun.edu/~hcedp007/Kalff-1991.pdf.

2. Fred Rogers, *You Are Special: Neighborly Words of Wisdom from Mister Rogers* (Penguin, 1995), 47.

3. Madeleine L'Engle, *A Circle of Quiet* (Open Road Media, 2016), 12.

4. Margaret Guenther, *Toward Holy Ground* (Cowley Publications, 1995), 69.

5. *Merriam-Webster's Collegiate Dictionary*, under "imagination" (Merriam-Webster, Inc., 2003).

6. Modeled after New Zealand poet Glenn Colquhoun's poem of the same name. See "Playing God," Jason Goroncy, December 31, 2016, https://jasongoroncy.com/2016/12/31/playing-god/.

7. Gregory A. Boyd, *Seeing Is Believing: Experience Jesus Through Imaginative Prayer* (Baker Books, 2004), 108.

Chapter 9 Flesh and Bone

1. Walt Whitman, *Leaves of Grass* (Oxford University Press, 1990), 21.

2. Bessel van der Kolk, *The Body Keeps the Score: Brain, Mind, and Body in the Healing of Trauma* (Penguin, 2014), 97.

3. Thanks to Rebecca Letterman of Embodiment Consulting Services for our phone conversation and for giving me this language. For more information, visit www.embodimentconsulting.com.

4. "They'll Know We Are Christians," lyrics by Peter Scholtes (© 1966 F.E.L. Publications, assigned to The Lorenz Corp., 1991).

5. Sebastian Ruiz-Blais, Michele Orini, and Elaine Chew, "Heart Rate Variability Synchronizes When Non-Experts Vocalize Together," *Frontiers in Physiology* 11 (September 2020), https://doi.org/10.3389/fphys.2020.00762.

6. James K. A. Smith, *You Are What You Love: The Spiritual Power of Habit* (Brazos Press, 2016), 3.

Chapter 10 Holding History

1. Ralph Waldo Emerson, "The Complete Works of Ralph Waldo Emerson: Letters and Social Aims [Vol. 8]," *The Complete Works of Ralph Waldo Emerson*, University of Michigan Library Digital Collections, accessed November 13, 2025, https://name.umdl.umich.edu/4957107.0008.001.

2. "Take My Life, and Let It Be," lyrics by Francis Ridley Havergal (1874).

3. Northumbria Community, "Morning Prayer," in *Celtic Daily Prayer: Prayers and Readings From the Northumbria Community* (HarperCollins, 2002), 18–19. Used by permission.

4. *The Book of Common Prayer* and Douglas McKelvey's Every Moment Holy collections are excellent sources of liturgical prayers. For more information about the latter, see www.everymomentholy.com/about-the-series.

5. Ignatius of Loyola, *Spiritual Exercises*, 103.

Chapter 11 Praying in the Dark

1. Oscar Wilde, *De Profundis* (Methuen and Co., 1913), 5.

2. Lisa Ann Moss Degrenia, "Order of Worship for a Blue Christmas Service (also Known as a Longest Night Service)," *Rev. Lisa Degrenia* (blog), November 26, 2024, https://revlisad.com/order-of-worship-for-a-blue-christmas-service-also-known-as-a-longest-night-service-2/. Used by permission.

3. "Sometimes I Feel Like a Motherless Child: Negro Spiritual," arranged by H. T. Burleigh (G. Ricordi, 1919), [notated music] retrieved from the Library of Congress, www.loc.gov/item/2009536943/.

4. George MacDonald, *Adela Cathcart—The Complete Fantasy Tales Series: The Light Princess, The Shadows, Christmas Eve, The Giant's Heart, The Broken Swords, The Cruel Painter, The Castle and Many More*, Kindle ed. (e-artnow, 2018), loc. 22.

5. Eugene Peterson, "Foreword," in Michael Card, *A Sacred Sorrow: Reaching Out to God in the Lost Language of Lament* (NavPress, 2014), 11.

6. M. E. Thibodeaux, *God's Voice Within: The Ignatian Way to Discover God's Will* (Loyola Press, 2010), 99.

Chapter 12 The Corner of Third and Vine

1. Henri J. M. Nouwen with Michael J. Christensen and Rebecca J. Laird, *Discernment: Reading the Signs of Daily Life* (HarperOne, 2013), 67.

2. William A. Barry, SJ, and W. J. Connolly, *The Practice of Spiritual Direction* (HarperCollins, 1982), 109.

3. Commonly attributed to Meister Eckhart (1260–1328).

4. Rainer Maria Rilke, *Letters to a Young Poet* (Dover Publications, 2012), 35.

5. Richard Rohr, *Falling Upward: A Spirituality for the Two Halves of Life* (Jossey-Bass, 2011), 6.

6. Thomas Merton, "The Merton Prayer," *Reflections*, January 1, 1970, https://reflections.yale.edu/article/seize-day-vocation-calling-work/merton-prayer.

Chapter 13 The Fallow Season

1. Kurt Vonnegut, *Player Piano* (Scribner, 1952), 82.

2. Katherine May, *Wintering: The Power of Rest and Retreat in Difficult Times* (Penguin, 2020), 14.

3. Thomas Merton, *Contemplative Prayer* (Image, 2014), 70.

4. Laura Kauffman, *Carolina Clay: A Collection of Poems on Love and Loss* (Dustlings Press, 2019), 75.

LAURA KAUFFMAN, MA, is a spiritual director and writer whose work explores the presence of God in everyday life. Drawing from the Christian contemplative tradition, she accompanies others in listening for God and responding to his invitation. She has published three collections of poetry that examine the holy edge of ordinary things. Laura lives with her family in the Midwest, where she practices spiritual direction and continues to write.